STUC...

"I like this approach. Dave handily debunks a lot of mythologies about history."

—**Grant Horner,** professor of Renaissance and Reformation Studies, The Master's University

"This is an extremely valuable book on the art of reading history. There are a number of good books out there on this subject that deal with the mechanics (how to cite footnotes and how to prepare a bibliography, etc.). This volume, though, is focused on what makes for wise usage of this valuable repository of knowledge that we call history. Recent events have shown that we all need to be better at understanding the past than we have been, and this book has nugget after nugget of wisdom on how to gain such an understanding. A five-star rating!"

—**Michael Haykin,** chair and professor of Church History, The Southern Baptist Theological Seminary

"Dave is a historical evangelical with a firm grasp of his indebtedness to the great Christian minds in the whole church through the ages. Both his mind and his heart will provide an edifying challenge to those who come into contact with his ministry."

—**Tom Nettles,** retired professor of Historical Theology, The Southern Baptist Theological Seminary

"David Moore's interview questions were focused and relevant. He has a unique ability to draw out answers from the interviewee that go beyond the usual clichés and boilerplate. I found the experience of being interviewed by him to be stimulating. It helped me focus on the main points I tried to get across in my book."

—**James McPherson,** Pulitzer Prize–winning historian, Princeton University

"In the hands of David Moore, history becomes so much more than simply dates and dead people. Instead, as he loves what he loves in front of his readers, history comes alive—and the learning of history becomes vital, the very foundation of wisdom and discernment. I highly recommend this handbook to life and learning."

—**George Grant,** pastor and prolific author

"Dave did his homework, asked all the right questions, and was a pleasure to sit down with. He's a real pro."

—**the late Tony Horwitz,** Pulitzer Prize–winning author and historian

"I find Dave's writing extremely compelling. He has produced a work that is scholarly, convincing, and practical. *Stuck in the Present* challenges me to expand my own knowledge of history along with helping my students counteract the postmodern ideas permeating our culture."

—**Diane Keller,** founder, Legacy Community Christian School

"Good historical thinking is absolutely necessary if we Christians are to have a better understanding of ourselves and the culture we are trying to reach with the gospel. David Moore understands this. His thoughts about history should be heeded by congregations everywhere."

—**John Fea,** professor of History, Messiah College

STUCK IN THE PRESENT

STUCK IN THE PRESENT

HOW HISTORY FREES + FORMS CHRISTIANS

David George Moore

Foreword by Carl R. Trueman

LEAFWOOD
PUBLISHERS
an imprint of Abilene Christian University Press

STUCK IN THE PRESENT

How History Frees and Forms Christians

LEAFWOOD
PUBLISHERS
an imprint of Abilene Christian University Press

ISBN 978-1-68426-460-5

Printed in the United States of America

Cataloging-in-Publication Data is on file at the Library of Congress, Washington, DC.

Cover design by ThinkPen Design, LLC
Interior text design by Sandy Armstrong, Strong Design

Leafwood Publishers is an imprint of Abilene Christian University Press
ACU Box 29138
Abilene, Texas 79699

1-877-816-4455
www.leafwoodpublishers.com

21 22 23 24 25 26 / 7 6 5 4 3 2 1

This book is dedicated to Scot McKnight.

During the first iteration of the Jesus Creed *blog (the Beliefnet days), Scot consistently interacted with me. It is unusual for a productive scholar like Scot to interact with his readers. Those of you who comment on blogs know how rare this is. Not only did Scot respond to many of my comments, but he was willing to receive pushback when we disagreed. You can appreciate why the invitation to be a regular contributor to Scot's blog was an easy decision.*

CONTENTS

ACKNOWLEDGMENTS

To those who have instilled in me a deep love for history:

Professor Chris Smith of Arizona State University, a truly scintillating teacher of American history.

Professor John Hannah of Dallas Theological Seminary, whose inimitable wit and honesty make history come alive.

Professors Tom Nettles and John Woodbridge of Trinity Evangelical Divinity School, whose teaching, coupled with a genuine interest in me personally, were a great encouragement.

Professors Robert Wilken of the University of Virginia; George Marsden of the University of Notre Dame; Wilfred McClay of the University of Oklahoma; James McPherson of Princeton University; Timothy Larsen of Wheaton College; Randall Balmer of Dartmouth College; Lanier Burns of Dallas Theological Seminary; Roger Lundin of Wheaton College; Dennis Okholm of Azusa Pacific University; Daniel Taylor, retired from Bethel University; Ralph Wood of Baylor University; Gerald McDermott and Doug Sweeney, both of

Beeson Divinity School; Carl Trueman of Grove City College; Gerald Sittser of Whitworth University; and Michael Haykin of Southern Seminary—my wonderfully responsive "teachers from afar."

Kurt and Susie Richardson, whose love of history served as an early catalyst for my own. Kurt and I have been friends for forty years. We share the same birthday, separated by three years. No one has encouraged me more or made more deposits for good in my life than Kurt.

Danny Smith, whose friendship, love of history, and offhand comment motivated me to put this material together.

Greg and Mary Jane Grooms of Hill House at the University of Texas at Austin. Along with many other things, I have taught this material at Hill House. My wife and I are deeply grateful to the Grooms for the invitation to be back teaching *and* learning in a university setting. The students are a true delight!

I am grateful to my friends Bill and Diana Bridgman and Scott Shadrach. Each one gave input on an earlier version of the manuscript. At a much later stage, I invoked the help of two friends, Dr. Dave McCoy and Dave Yocum. Both Daves have keen eyes. All five of these friends are gentle and wise readers. As authors always say, and for good reason, whatever deficiencies remain are my responsibility alone.

Many thanks to Professor Shane Wood for enthusiastically recommending me to his publisher. And speaking of publishers, I am grateful to the Press Director of Leafwood Publishers and Abilene Christian University Press, Dr. Jason Fikes. Jason prodded me to tweak and add some material that made this book better. Mary Hardegree has been a delight to work with: quick to respond, competent, and gracious. Duane Anderson answered my many queries with a sure and steady hand. Rachel Paul delivered an impeccable copyedit. Kylie Kincaid, Taylor Humphrey, and Al Estrada helped with a myriad of other details.

For twenty-three years, I have written under the auspices of Two Cities Ministries. I am grateful to our board (Tim Taylor, Paul Van Allen, and Jon Werner) for their encouragment and commitment to what we are seeking to do. The many friends who support Two Cities are a constant source of encouragement. My ever-steady and uber-competent assistant, Barb Miaso, has helped in too many ways to count.

Finally, there is my family: I love that our sons, David and Chris, like to discuss issues of substance. I am grateful to now add David's new bride, Reese, to the family. My wife, Doreen, is a trained historian and writer. She has taught me the most—about many areas of life.

FOREWORD

Philip Rieff commented that forgetfulness has become the fundamental shape of higher education. His point, connected to his broader understanding of culture, was that the elites of our day are no longer committed to the transmission of the institutions, customs, and values of the past to the present and thence to the future. Instead, we live in an age of intentional iconoclasm of such things, fueled by a cultural amnesia that is not so much marked by accidental absent mindedness as by a deliberate forgetfulness. And this forgetfulness is itself based upon a widely held hubristic notion that the past is at most a salutary warning to the present, a tale of exploitation, ignorance, and mediocrity.

Yet our identities, our notions of who we are, our intuitions of how to relate to the world around us, and our moral imaginations are all anchored in the past. Yes, we make our own history but, as Marx portentously commented, we do not make the history that we choose. And that is why knowledge of history—more than that, knowledge of how to think historically—is so important. And why the forgetfulness of our current culture is so potentially harmful. We need to understand the past, not so much in order to avoid its mistakes (though that is much to be desired) as to understand who we are.

This is where Dave Moore's book will prove so helpful. In it, he offers thoughtful reflections on the historical task, and specifically on how this is of importance to Christians as they seek to be both faithful members of the church and thoughtful members of society at large. Remarkably for such a small book, Dave covers some of the most difficult questions in approaching history. How do we move beyond being trapped in the present? Why is the past still relevant? How much can we really know about the past? And underlying all is a quiet, gentlemanly, though firm, polemic against those who would argue that all a Christian really needs to do is read the Bible. That might be enough to take one to heaven; but as Moore shows, it is not enough to allow one to be an informed and self-aware sojourner in the earthly city.

Finally, in the appendices, Dave does what he does best: interviews a number of historians about how they see their own role in this, how they understand their own task in history, and what significance they see history as having for society in general. In a year when debates are occurring about history, about national origins, and about what of that past should be on display in the present, these closing reflections are particularly thought-provoking.

Dave Moore has been a friend for some years. I have always found his writings to be helpful and challenging, even on the odd occasion when I find myself disagreeing with him. He is a scholar and a gentleman, a model of the kind of engaged thinker we need so badly and yet have so few of. I hope this book will help readers not only think historically but also reflect upon how important civility is in our troubled and contentious times.

—Carl R. Trueman
Christian Theologian and Ecclesiastical Historian
Professor of Biblical and Religious Studies, Grove City College

CHAPTER ONE

STUCK IN THE PRESENT

A church which has lost its memory of the past can only wander about aimlessly in the present and despair of its future. Having lost its identity, it will lose its mission and its hope as well. **—David C. Steinmetz**

Those who cannot remember the past are condemned to repeat it. **—George Santayana**

History is more or less bunk. It's tradition. We don't want tradition. We want to live in the present, and the only history that is worth a tinker's damn is the history that we make today. **—Henry Ford**

I am finishing the final edits of this book during the coronavirus (COVID-19) pandemic. Like many Americans, I am quarantined in my house. As I write this, we are in the sixth month of this crisis, and no one knows how long it will last or how difficult the days ahead will be. Some are willing to speculate, but many of these pronouncements don't seem to be worth any serious consideration.

To some, writing a book in the midst of a global crisis may seem like a bad use of time. I disagree and take my cue from G. K. Chesterton, who said there is always a great need for thoughtful people, especially during trying times. The thoughtful person, according to Chesterton, may prove to be the most helpful. Those who do not like to think make decisions based on things that commonly work. Thoughtful people will consider options outside established norms or patterns. In some small way, I hope this book vindicates Chesterton's sage counsel.

Let me say a few words about the title, *Stuck in the Present: How History Frees and Forms Christians*. I find many Christians uninterested in the study of history. This lack of enthusiasm, as I will argue throughout this book, is not only a shame but limits one's formation as a Christian. Ironically, paying attention to what is transpiring in the present does not give the proper context to evaluate what is *actually* transpiring in the present. We need a longer view to evaluate and make sense of the present. We need a grounding in the full sweep of human events. Greater familiarity with the lived experience of our fellow humans throughout the ages gives us better tools for living wisely in our own time. Growing in our appreciation for history frees us from the shackles of modern-day hucksters who try to convince us that the present is all that matters. As we will see, history frees and forms Christians in a myriad of wonderful ways.

A continual study (and our study of the past should be lifelong!) makes one less vulnerable to whatever fads are in vogue at present. Studying history offers wisdom for every imaginable situation we encounter under the sun. Studying the past puts us in contact with people whose handling of their own challenges supplies us with a much-needed perspective for our own.

It is great fun to have those "aha moments" when we begin to connect the dots between various events. This takes place, for example, when one makes the connection that the growing democratic spirit in America of the early nineteenth century not only was realized in the so-called political arena but was increasingly embodied in the working assumptions of the church.[1]

Let me add another example from my engagement with Voltaire's fascinating book *Candide.* During my reading, I wondered whether the wealthy Venetian character by the name of Pococurante, who said he was "tired of both beautiful women and paintings," happened to be a good example of ennui or what we Americans have come to understand as boredom. Boredom, like everything else, has a history! I decided to reach out to Professor Patricia Spacks who wrote *Boredom: The Literary History of a State of Mind.* Professor Spacks wrote back and confirmed that Pococurante was indeed a "classic example of boredom."

These kinds of connections are thrilling to make and give us a deeper appreciation for how the human story, what we call *history,* is intertwined in myriad ways. According to neuroscientist Daniel Levitin, we are hardwired (he thinks due to evolution; I think due to God) to name our world. Not only are we hardwired to do so, but we delight in doing so:

> This innate passion for naming and categorizing can be brought into stark relief by the fact that *most* of the naming we do in the plant world might be considered strictly unnecessary. Out of the 30,000 edible plants thought to exist on earth, just eleven account for 93% of all that humans eat: oats, corn, rice, wheat, potatoes, yucca (also called tapioca or cassava), sorghum, millet, beans, barley, and rye. *Yet our brains evolved to receive a pleasant shot of dopamine when we learn*

something new and again when we classify it systematically into an ordered structure.[2]

With respect to history, it is easy to see that classification (say, knowing some of the differences between the Renaissance and the Enlightenment) provides a necessary scaffolding to keep learning *and* delighting in one's deeper understanding of the world. We were designed by God to better understand the world we inhabit, so it is particularly sad when Christians lose their curiosity to learn. We will explore this topic further in due course.

Advantages of This Study

Throughout this book, you will find regular sections that highlight the various advantages that come from applying oneself to the disciplined study of history. These will be tagged as "Benefits to You and Your Ministry." Here you will gain a growing sense of the benefits that come from the study of history. Your own life will be enriched, and you will be better equipped as a Christian to engage the complexities of our world.

The study of history certainly offers plenty of drama and supplies ample wisdom. There are, however, potholes along the way. *Stuck in the Present* offers guidance for those who want to benefit from the riches of studying the past while not falling prey to some common errors.

One of the most frequent questions that an author faces when writing a book, and one I have already received, revolves around one's primary audience. It is okay to also have a secondary audience, but literary orthodoxy demands that you decide on your main audience.

Writing guru William Zinsser offered sound advice to popular writer Donald Miller with respect to "obsessing over one's target audience." Zinsser's recommendation was to "write for yourself and assume that there are readers just like you." Miller found this counsel both illuminating and liberating, and I also resonate with Zinsser's advice. However, I am aware that many will not be so easily persuaded, so I will just stick with convention here. I am writing first and foremost for nonspecialists, especially Christians who are willing to consider how the study of history can benefit their relationship with God. I also hope there are things in these pages that will be of benefit to those who spend much of their time studying and teaching history.

My Approach

The process of recording, writing, and teaching about history is selective (see Chapter Three). One chooses to cover certain people and events while leaving out others. My own approach when I teach history in a Sunday school class or for a parachurch group follows three broad criteria: (1) what best moves the story forward, (2) what areas I have studied the most, and (3) what areas are of special interest to those attending my classes. Criteria two and three lead me to give greater coverage to the Puritans, challenges to the Christian faith in America during the nineteenth century, and several trends affecting the church in the United States today. I spend considerable time on Saint Augustine because of his massive influence and how he speaks with such profound relevance to our current cultural moment.[3] Though I emphasize certain people and events more than others, I work hard to be accurate and balanced in terms of what I do end up covering.

Eminent historian Donald Kagan said that simply reporting events, even with a careful eye for accuracy, does not necessarily mean the discipline of history is being represented or followed. Doing this only makes one a *chronicler* of events. A historian, on the other hand, must show *why* the selected subject matter is important. In detailing why certain events and persons are picked over others, the study of history also has a philosophical thrust.[4]

While interviewing historian Wilfred McClay, I asked him what he thought about Kagan's reflections on the nature of historical writing.[5] McClay very much agreed with Kagan's point about the difference between writing history and being a mere chronicler of events. McClay made it clear that there is a "genuine creativity involved in the making of a historical narrative." McClay underscored that we don't want to fall prey to an "arbitrary creativity," where the best evidence is bypassed or treated recklessly. The proportions of our account must reflect our best attempts to reconstruct what took place. McClay voiced the need for aspiring and established historians to not only look for what confirms our own view of what transpired; we should also look for evidence that undermines what we think occurred. In other words, all should seek to have the courage "to yield your thesis, and revise and rethink on the grounds of what you've found out."

Thus this process of selection cannot be avoided. It will take place no matter who is telling the story. With respect to the interview I conducted with McClay, his own use of the historical record in his book *Land of Hope* is very different from the events and people that Howard Zinn found noteworthy for his best-selling *A People's History of the United States*. Both

McClay and Zinn could be presenting a reliable account of our past—though I do not personally believe this is the case. There are ways to assess who is handling the historical record more responsibly. Much of the rest of this book will address what careful handling of the historical record entails. I have written this primer to provide tools that offer greater discernment with respect to the writing of responsible history.

Good historians, and those who know how to spot good historical writing, are willing to let the story they are telling be challenged. For example, someone who extols the history of the United States as "miraculous" must honestly reckon with the harsh realities of slavery, the poor treatment of Native Americans, and the increasing cynicism about its government from a growing number of its citizenry. One may be able to describe the American experiment as "miraculous" and still write responsible history if these injustices, and more besides, are carefully considered in the narration of the story. If a historian considers these injustices honestly but still chooses to employ the word "miraculous," then he or she will have to define what that word means and does not mean.

Benefits to You and Your Ministry

The good news about all this is that we can develop the skills needed for determining whether a historical account is given fair treatment. We need not fear that we will be stuck in some bewildering maze of uncertainty about what "really happened." We can be confident about discovering where the truth lies. A general accuracy about periods, people, and events is achievable,[6] but there is hard work to do. As Christians, we have a great advantage here. Our Christian faith tells us to love the truth. This should motivate us to steer clear of superficial and shoddy work.

One alarming trend is the growing disparity between so-called progressive and so-called conservative Christians about a whole host of issues. These differences revolve around such things as sexual ethics, the environment, the nature of capitalist economies, and so much more. One illustration I like to use for these debates is the difference between a barnacle and a boat. Barnacles, you may know, are those sticky crustaceans that affix themselves to the bottom of the boat. If you fail to flip the boat and scrape them off (some use newer technologies for this process), those little critters will eat into the hull and make your boat no longer seaworthy. Flipping a boat and cleaning off sticky crustaceans is not sexy work. It is much more fun to set out sailing or head out on some fishing adventure.

I invite people to think of the Christian faith as the boat. Barnacles are the things we may believe, but they have little or nothing to do with the Christian faith. A good example here comes from my four years of part-time teaching at a Christian school. There were several rules governing things such as proper clothing and jewelry. Some of these things made sense, but I get nervous whenever man-made rules are multiplied. I remember Philip Yancey asking whether the 600-plus commandments given to the Jews in biblical times made them more obedient to God. My other concern with all the rules at this fine school was the mistake that too many parents, students, teachers, and administrators made. I came up with an alliteration that encapsulated my concern: Watch out when human *preferences* slowly become *priorities* that slowly, but surely, are treated as biblical *precepts*.

Christians who are willing to do the hard work of knowing the past will be better able to determine what is a proverbial barnacle and what is the boat. So-called progressive Christians tend to be comfortable with flipping the boat and commencing to scrape. But their temptation is to scrape too much and therefore compromise the integrity of the Christian faith. More so-called conservative Christians tend to steer clear of flipping the boat altogether: "The boat looks great, so let's keep using it as it is." For example, there may be resistance to pondering whether capitalism has any sinister elements that should be guarded against. In fact, for some, considering whether there are *any* harmful aspects of capitalism can be a threatening prospect. It may be a barnacle, but we just don't want to acknowledge it as such. We are happy to sail on without scraping.

Christians who are willing to wrestle honestly with the past will not only be equipped to have better conversations with fellow Christians about their differences; they will also be better equipped to engage thoughtfully with those who do not adhere to the Christian faith.

Important Things to Remember about Learning

There are several matters that should be considered when it comes to the study of any field or discipline. Desiring to deepen our understanding is a noble thing, but there are important factors to keep in mind. It also should be said that a regular reminder of these things is indeed wise, no matter how competent or far along we are in a certain area of study. The following is certainly not an exhaustive list, but I do believe it covers some of the more important aspects we must keep in mind for properly learning about any subject.

Learning Involves Hard Work

There's no doubt that anything worthwhile takes blood, sweat, and tears. Whatever one thinks of Malcolm Gladwell's idea that "10,000 hours of practice" are needed to be world-class in any field, we all know that hard work over a long period is indispensable for high-level achievement.

Sadly, many Christians no longer consider the value of such effort when it comes to learning. Many of us gladly expend great effort to shave a stroke or two off our golf handicap or perhaps make a bit more money, but giving diligent attention to learning is increasingly rare among us. This kind of lazy anti-intellectualism does not seem to be any better whether someone is religious or not. (Orthodox Jews may be the rare exception here.)

If most of us are willing to stay up all night binge-watching a season or several episodes of our favorite television show, then we surely can devote more time to learning. In this book, I will make the case for learning history, though there are many other important subjects that are worthy of our attention.

For more than forty years as a Christian, I have heard learning widely demeaned among my fellow Christians in subtle and not-so-subtle ways. I have heard it in churches, in various ministries I have been intimately involved in, and among Christians in the business community.[7] "It is not practical." "It hurts one's zeal for God." "It makes you arrogant." These, and other objections, are typically offered as warnings against going deeper into one's understanding. And there is also much confusion about the relationship between wisdom and knowledge. We'll return to this topic and the idea of vulnerability to arrogance in a bit. Adding to this sad state of affairs is that these kinds of comments have come from many people with college degrees. For these individuals, education served as more a means of getting a certain type of job rather than the doorway to lifelong learning. Various studies reveal how little college-educated Americans read. My own interactions with a variety of adults, most of whom are college graduates, illustrates this low regard for reading—especially challenging books that stretch the mental muscles.

When I fly or am waiting at the DMV, I try to glance around to see who is reading. Typically, very few are reading physical books. Some read on electronic devices, but movie watching, listening to music, and playing various games are the dominant activities. On a recent trip to the DMV, I was stunned by how many folks just stared off into the distance—and the stare did not look like it included any thoughtful meditation!

Since there is so much confusion about the importance of learning among American Christians, it is helpful for us to get our bearings by looking at some of our country's history. I have left out several factors in the following sketch (remember what I said about selection), but I do think the following overview will offer further clarity as to why so many Christians are skeptical about the importance of learning.

Learning Involves Both the "Head" and the "Heart" (A Short History)

Significant changes have transpired in our country's history when it comes to how we envision the role of the pastor. From seventeenth-century Puritanism until today, we find that the shifts in the pastor's role are indeed dramatic. For whatever flaws Puritan ministers had,[8] it is clear that many of them were giants in terms of their intellect and piety. Their "heads and hearts" were both vitally engaged, not to mention their hands. With respect to their "hands," it is interesting to note that Benjamin Franklin, though not holding to Cotton Mather's theology, was very impressed by how this Puritan pastor conducted his life. It is also interesting to note that Puritan ministers were not just viewed as the spiritual leaders of their time; many were considered the *educational* leaders of society as well.[9] Cotton Mather was certainly emblematic of this model.

The value of a learned clergy has increasingly lost currency in our country's history. Fortunately, I know several pastors who are people of deep learning *and* warm hearts. On the other side of the ledger, I am sorry to say I have had many conversations with pastors who openly disparage the importance of learning. I could tell many stories like this but will limit myself to two.

When I was interviewing for a pastoral position, there was one evangelical pastor who said he would love for me to assume the role if I did one thing: refrain from talking about theology with the congregation. He said we could talk about theology *in his office*, but he wanted me to steer clear of having those conversations publicly. No kidding. I know this sounds like hyperbole, but this terribly misguided pastor was quite earnest. With thinly veiled condescension, he went on to tell me that theology would just confuse people in the pews. This pastor may be more extreme than many others, but I am afraid he is not alone.

Another incident took place after I preached a sermon at an evangelical church in New York. When I was done, the senior pastor thanked me and then proceeded to tell me that he also used to be excited about preaching the Bible but had since found a new love. (He did not exactly call it a "new love," but that's what was clearly communicated.) In his doctorate of ministry program,[10] he found that the study of Freud, Jung, and others had allowed him to help people "unlike anything else."

Since I believe all truth is God's truth, I would agree that important insights can come from secular thinkers, but one needs to be discerning when sifting the wheat from the chaff. People outside the Christian faith can offer us sorely needed perspectives that we are too blind to see. Christian philosopher Merold Westphal has helped me with this as much as anyone. Westphal does a terrific job showing that the likes of Freud, Nietzsche, and Marx, the so-called masters of suspicion, raise important concerns that those within the church sometimes fail to notice.[11] Perhaps we Christians are somewhat aware that these problem areas exist but find them too threatening to broach. Either way, skeptics and all sorts of people outside the Christian faith are wise to have as conversation partners. It should be stated that we need to be careful about *whom* we pick and *when* we engage with them. We need not have too many of these folks in our lives, since time is valuable and there is much to learn about in our own Christian tradition. However, I've found many men and women I respect taking the time to engage with skeptics. They want to truly know how well their Christian faith fares in the face of those who raise serious criticisms. Timing is crucial here, so *when* we choose to interact with skeptics requires wisdom. If we are not firmly grounded in the Christian faith, then it is not yet time to converse with or read the work of skeptics. Notwithstanding these concerns, having a few critics who push us, if these are chosen wisely and at the right time, can yield great benefits.

I have benefitted greatly over the years from my engagement with various critics—none more so than Ralph Waldo Emerson.[12] He has probably been my most helpful interlocutor. He regularly points out things that make me wince, but he forces me to ask questions I might not otherwise ask. For example, he made me wrestle more honestly with what true belief entails. His searing comments about ministers who don't seem to believe what they are preaching about have forced me to evaluate my own teaching and sometimes preaching. I find myself wondering what Emerson would think if he heard me preach. It is ultimately only important what God thinks when it comes to anything I do, but Emerson offers some candid commentary that forces me to think in a way that is unlike any preaching book I've read. And I have read several valuable books on preaching.

Back to our minister in New York who was reading Freud and Jung. His mistake was not found in reading non-Christian thinkers. His mistake was in deciding that the Bible, theology, and history were no longer of much help in comparison. And though this minister picked some good conversation partners, he did not have an adequate grounding in history and theology to see the problems inherent in his glad acceptance of Freudian and Jungian thought.

One could also add here that most pastors choose not to keep up with the Greek and/or Hebrew they previously learned. Language study is widely and openly declared to be impractical. This seems due to more than just the time demands of pastoral ministry.

When I ask ministers and other Christian leaders what books they have been reading, I rarely hear history books of real substance mentioned. Biographies are mentioned, which is terrific, but serious books on history are rarely mentioned. The books typically listed are books on ministry strategy, leadership, popular spirituality, cultural analysis, and psychology. These dominate the responses.[13]

On the other side of the ledger, we certainly have learned pastors, but some of these do not handle the messy details of pastoral ministry very well. I have known some who even steer clear of hospital visitation and crisis counseling. These tasks get offloaded to others so this kind of "minister" can simply focus on preaching. I even know of one church where a pastoral candidate made it clear to those interviewing him that he was *only* coming to preach. Of course there are some ministers who gladly engage with those in need, but they are not always the most thoughtful in their approach. Thus I don't think it is a stretch to say we have reached the unenviable place described by one American minister in 1853 as "an impression, somewhat general, that an intellectual clergyman is deficient in piety, and that an eminently pious minister is deficient in intellect."[14] Again, I am happy to say that my own pastors and many others I know combine a thoughtful approach with a warm heart for people. I am merely making the point that this is all too uncommon.

Let's go back to the Puritans for a moment. They believed "the head and the heart" were crucial for spiritual maturity.[15] Theology and spirituality were inextricably linked.[16] In our time, that connection strikes many as strange, unattractive, and no longer relevant.

Today we find far too many pastors who are so enamored with church growth strategies or personal piety that they are unable to address the knottier questions many in their congregations have. We are living in a time where things such as changing sexual mores, technology, and complex ethical issues raised by medical breakthroughs should easily persuade us that learning is one of the most pressing priorities of the church. Sadly, this does not seem to be the prevailing view, though wonderful exceptions give us hope.[17] The complexity of our modern world clearly demands ongoing education for *all* Christians. A growing knowledge of history affords the kind of discernment that is essential for our own cultural moment. As Timothy George likes to say, there are many important things we ought to know that happened between the death of Jesus and the birth of our grandmother!

If pastors and other Christian leaders demean, devalue, or downplay the importance of learning—and here we are speaking specifically of learning history—then we should not be surprised when many who look to them for guidance follow their lead. Christians who are ignorant of history are hardly going to be effective witnesses to the world when they step outside their door.

The so-called battle between the head and the heart is one we must cease fighting. It is an unnecessary and, more importantly, harmful fight. Our knowledge of history ought to fuel a greater desire to love God and love others. Growing in one's knowledge of history helps us in big ways, but there are certainly dangers involved with all sorts of learning.

Frank Gaebelein once said, "Education without character is a dangerous thing."[18] "Knowledge is power," as Bacon's famous aphorism declares. It is seductive with its lure of mastery over others. I have learned about this temptation several times and keep learning it. I'll give you one example here, but I could offer many more.

Years ago, I preached a sermon at my home church, giving a strong critique of a well-known "health-wealth" preacher. I think my comments were appropriate, but there was something important I still had to learn. My omnicompetent assistant, Barb, came to me a few weeks after I preached this sermon and mentioned that someone in our church was extremely offended by what I had said. It took a bit of effort to ascertain who the person was, since the complaint came to Barb through various layers of people. Once we knew, I gave this person a call, but before I picked up the phone, I gathered my thoughts and prayed. I decided to meditate on 1 and 2 Timothy. It did not take long for the Holy Spirit to convict me. I landed on 1 Timothy 1:5: "But the goal of our instruction is love from a pure heart, from a good conscience, and from a sincere faith" (NASB). God's Spirit spoke this to my spirit: "You know a whole lot more than Bernard [not his real name], but you need to make sure that love is your motivation for correcting his poor understanding rather than just wanting to win a debate." James K. A. Smith puts it well:

> Augustine would give a name to this kind of disordered relationship to wisdom and learning: *curiositas*. Curiosity for Augustine is not the spirit of inquiry we prize and encourage; rather, it is a kind of quest for knowledge that doesn't know what it's for—a knowing for knowing's sake, we might say, or perhaps more to the point, knowing for the sake of being known as someone who knows. For Augustine, the *reason* I want to know is an indicator of the sort of love that motivates my learning. Am I learning in order to grow, learning in order to know who and how to love? Or am I learning in order to wield power, get noticed, be seen as smart, be "in the know"?[19]

I was sobered by the Holy Spirit using God's Word in this way to correct me. I am glad to say that my friendship with Bernard was strengthened by our conversation. I am not glad to report that since this time I have allowed my frustration and ego to get the best of me in correcting others. Knowing a lot about any subject can be dangerous indeed. The opposite, knowing little and being very zealous, also has its own traps. (We'll return to this topic a little later in the section "Knowledge Is Practical.")

Bernard of Clairvaux wisely said, "There are those who desire to acquire knowledge for its own sake—and this is a base vanity. But there are others who desire to have it edify others—and this is charity."[20] Guarding against making knowledge an idol is commendable and wise. However, the pitfalls of a superficial understanding of history also have disastrous consequences. Dorothy Sayers was incredulous at how many Christians could get excited about worshipping God when their understanding of him was so shallow.[21] In contrast to the boredom Sayers observed among many in their engagement with Christian doctrine, she trenchantly declared that "dogma is the drama."[22] In fact, her play *The Zeal of Thy House* was a "dramatic presentation of a few fundamental Christian dogmas—in particular, the application to human affairs of the doctrine of the Incarnation." When people applauded Sayers for *her* genius and novelty in writing such a play, she would correct them by saying that her work was strongly dependent on Christian doctrine.[23] And these great doctrines of the Christian faith are all anchored in history. We must keep this in mind. The Christian faith is firmly grounded in history. This is one of the things that C. S. Lewis found so compelling. It gave credibility to the claims of the Christian faith and was instrumental in Lewis's conversion.[24]

I have a confession to make here. All this talk about the head and the heart has been somewhat of a ruse. Yes, many find the head and the heart to be regularly at odds—even antagonistic to one another. We can all appreciate how what we supposedly know does not always translate to what we do. Unfortunately, the way we frame this problem is also problematic.

Our commonly accepted way of describing the battle between the head and the heart has distorted our perceptions about the importance of learning. The Scriptures, as Lesslie Newbigin carefully conveys,[25] present the problem differently—namely, that knowing is not true knowing without accompanying doing. In other words, if a person claims to "know God" but does not obey God's commands, then that person is a liar (1 John 2:4)—strong but clarifying language. Conversely, obedience to God shows that one truly knows him (1 John 2:5). Rightly did Jonathan Edwards warn when he said, "Holy affections do not have heat without light. Constantly there must be the information of the understanding, so that there is spiritual instruction which the mind receives as light or actual knowledge."[26] Here Edwards was advocating that all Christians, not just clergy, be committed to lifelong learning.

The knowing/doing dichotomy may owe some of its origin to Greek philosophy. Regardless of its origin, the children of Israel understood that true learning and doing were inextricably linked. For example, the knowledge that God is one (Deut. 6:4) is tied directly to love (Deut. 6:5). Adding confusion to this issue is the popular notion that the heart is simply an emotive organ. This is the way we typically view it in the West. It is better to see the heart as the mainspring of the will. To have God's commands on one's heart (Deut. 6:6) is to have them, so to speak, on one's will and mind.

Think about Paul's instruction to his beloved friend Timothy. Timothy was encouraged to pay close attention to both himself *and* his teaching (1 Tim. 4:16). The result of such godly vigilance was immensely practical: salvation for himself and his hearers. This connection between truly knowing something and obedience is modeled throughout the pages of the Bible. When Daniel grasped Jeremiah's prophecy that the impending destruction of Jerusalem applied to his generation, he immediately sought God through prayer and fasting (Dan. 9:2,3). On the other side of things, if God's commands are not practiced, it can impair one's ability to understand the deeper things of God (John 14:21). The Pharisees knew much about the Torah, but they made the fateful mistake of not knowing to whom the law pointed (John 5:39–47). As a result, one could argue they really did not know the law in any meaningful way.

One author adds that "[a]n accurate albeit awkward synonym for the biblical term 'heart' is 'motivational structure.'"[27] We should thus be vigilant to maintain the dynamic relationship Scripture presents between what we are learning and how that learning affects our lives.

Benefits to You and Your Ministry

The lesson to be learned from this brief background is that Christian education is not a purely cerebral endeavor. Since many Christians view it this way, the study of history (and other subjects) is wrongly believed to be only for "Christian eggheads." Diligent and intentional learning is viewed as a negotiable activity for a select few—a hobby of sorts for those so inclined.

Clearly, learning involves the intellect. There is no getting around that. But to suggest that Christian education is fundamentally a cerebral enterprise strips it of its moral and spiritual dimensions. The church and our culture, in general, are desperately in need of men and women who model the truth that the obedient are learners (Heb. 5:11–14). One friend reminded me that what we think influences the options we see, which in turn influences the choices we make.[28] The choices we make obviously influence the kind of life we live. This reminder underscores the practicality of careful thinking.

History certainly enriches one's life, but it also allows for greater effectiveness in ministering to a wide variety of people. For Christians with the bent of an activist, it is wise to remember that one's ability to minister can be greatly aided by deep learning. Lack of depth will limit how effectively one is able to engage with certain people.

Learning, when approached from a Christian framework, will always keep formation front and center. This is widely acknowledged by Christians as a noble end. What may be not as clear is understanding the *beauty* of truth.

In a fascinating book on the origins of the so-called political right and left, Yuval Levin contrasts Edmund Burke (a man of the right) with Thomas Paine (a man of the left).[29] Edmund Burke believed that institutions were worth preserving. He also believed that incremental change was wisest. Thomas Paine believed the opposite—that institutions have a short shelf life, so slower change is unwise. Paine espoused that revolution and upheaval are necessary. It is no surprise that his little book *Common Sense* would rally support for the American Revolution. For our purposes, it is interesting how Burke believed one should approach persuading someone like Paine about whether institutions are worth preserving. Since Burke believed that people are drawn to "novelty and excitement," it was critical to show the beauty of institutions.

I would give many of us Christians high marks for seeking to show the truthfulness of our faith but much lower marks for showing the beauty of our faith in Jesus.

> In our own day, we desperately need Christians who understand the truth but can also showcase its beauty.

Learning Requires Knowing How to Proceed as Learners

After surveying this brief history, some of you may remain uncertain as to your own ability to engage more thoughtfully with the Christian faith. Well, I have some very good news for all of us. Desire and effort[30] can make up quite a bit for a lack of raw intelligence, though using whatever intelligence one has been given is critical. We do well to remember these important words from renowned educator Frank Gaebelein: "The challenge of the Christian intellectual life is indeed great. But it is not an easy challenge. It costs to have a mind that is really dedicated to the Lord." Gaebelein did not pull his punches on the need to count the cost along with the huge benefits that come from the "discipline of self-restraint and plain hard work."[31]

Our expectations are currently far too low. In fact, I like to ask different people whether they go to church expecting to "be stretched intellectually." I purposely use the word "intellectually." I get odd looks. "What are you talking about, Dave? I go to church to worship God." Note well the assumption that is operative there. Worshipping God, it is assumed, has little to do with the mind. Worshipping God is somehow separate from how we think and view the world.

Finding time to be more intentional about learning is stymied for many of us by watching too much television. This is a major culprit responsible for wasting precious time. As a result, some decide to rid their homes entirely of television. Pastor

John Piper is one such individual. Others try to limit both the amount of time television is watched and maintain diligence as to the content. Whatever your convictions, this is an area for careful consideration, not passivity.

Watching too much television impedes learning . . . unless you apply the "Groucho principle." The inimitable Groucho Marx said, "I find television very educating. Every time somebody turns on the set, I go into the other room and read a book." David Frost also had some pungent words to offer about television: "Television is an invention that permits you to be entertained in your living room by people you wouldn't have in your home."[32]

Learning requires concentration and patience—not the kinds of things television fosters.[33] Aside from ubiquitous sensuality, there is also the banality of most television shows. Rapidly changing images force us to make a quick decision. We are unable to process properly as the rapidly changing images inhibit thoughtful reflection. Even the supposedly more serious shows like the local news now serve mainly to entertain. I remember watching our local news[34] and the two lead stories were Davy Jones of the Monkees band being picked up on a DWI and the sordid charges against Michael Jackson. When I first started writing this book,[35] the lead story (which trumped a story about five people being shot in a workplace rampage and another on Iran's nuclear threat) was the feud between Jay Leno and Conan O'Brien over *The Tonight Show*. This kind of thing is standard fare today on our media platforms. Both trivial and profound stories hit us with equal force. This phenomenon is what I like to call the "democratization of data."

Everything coming at us supposedly carries equal importance. How can one determine what is worth paying attention to? It is no wonder that enormously important issues like immigration and what wars are worth fighting immobilize us because their complexities demand long and focused study. The required study is not sexy. Sound bites will win out every time, and so most simply say whatever is on their mind. And since most minds are not full of solid study, we hear poorly formed ideas trying to masquerade as compelling thoughts.

The sheer amount of information deluging us causes even intelligent people to lose their way. Consider the humorous "experiment" that the late Neil Postman used to give to his colleagues at New York University:

> The experiment is best conducted in the morning when I see a colleague who appears not to be in possession of a copy of *The New York Times*. "Did you read the *Times* this morning?" I ask. If my colleague says, "Yes," there is no experiment that day. But if the answer is "No," the experiment can proceed. "You ought to check out Section C today," I say. "There's a fascinating article about a study done at the University of Minnesota." "Really? What's it all about?" is the usual reply. The choices at this point are almost endless, but there are two that produce rich results. The first: "Well, they did this study to find out what foods are best to eat for losing weight, and it turns out that a normal diet supplemented by chocolate eclairs eaten three times a day is the best approach. It seems that there's some special nutrient

> in the eclairs—encomial dioxin—that actually uses up calories at an incredible rate."
>
> The second changes the theme and, from the start, the university: "The neurophysiologists at Johns Hopkins have uncovered a connection between jogging and reduced intelligence. They tested more than twelve hundred people over a period of five years, and found that as the number of hours people jogged increased there was a statistically significant decrease in their intelligence. They don't know exactly why, but there it is."[36]

Postman went on to say that "about two-thirds" of his colleagues believe "or at least not wholly disbelieve" what he has told them. The funniest response comes from colleagues who say, "You know, I've heard something like that."[37] Some of us may be inclined to think that university professors are easier than most to fool, but the onslaught of data makes discerning the truth a challenge for all of us.

There is a way to navigate through these challenges, but we must avail ourselves of the best strategies. Among other things, we should ask wise people what books have been formative in their own life.

We also ought to expose ourselves to a variety of viewpoints. Again, I would want Christians to be strongly grounded in the Christian faith before doing this, but there should come a time when we challenge ourselves by exposure to diverse perspectives. When we had a television in our home, I regularly watched all three of the major cable news stations: MSNBC, CNN, and Fox. In the car, I regularly listen to both NPR and conservative talk radio. All have their biases, but it is good to force myself through the chaos to locate where the truth seems to lie. For the record, I do not always find this enjoyable. In fact, most of the time, *enjoyment* is not even close to the word I would use to describe my experience. I can report, however, that it has been beneficial in forcing me to think more deeply about the important issues of our day. For many, I would recommend reducing the amount of social media one ingests.[38] I am glad to not be on Facebook or Twitter. I rarely look at Facebook, but I do check out certain Twitter feeds. Sometimes I find things of value. But, many times, this information does not add anything of value to my life. If we could delete tweets with self-promotional ads and threads with inane discussions about things like what makes a great pizza, not to mention the outrage du jour, there would be much less tweeting taking place!

With all the silly, nonsubstantial stuff floating around, we can easily lose sight of what is important to know. I am regularly struck by how little of the important stuff many Christians have at their fingertips. I have even done some of my own informal polling to find out. For example, most Christians are unable to give a coherent reason for why they believe the books in the Bible are the Word of God. I have found that the basic historical details of the canon of Scripture are not always well understood, even by ministers. And this lack of understanding is not due to the material being difficult to understand. For example, with respect to the canon of Scripture, there are some clear and compelling answers to the typical critiques of skeptics.

The popular argument is that powerful bishops at the Council of Nicaea (325 AD) all but forced the books of the Bible on the rest of us for final inclusion into what we accept as the authoritative books or canon. Many responses could be given here. For example, there were churches in many different locales prior to Nicaea who already considered our New Testament books authoritative. There is also the Muratorian Canon, containing most of the books of the New Testament, which was solidified a hundred years prior to Nicaea. You do not find any Gnostic writings in it like the *Gospel of Thomas*. Powerful bishops were not doing something sinister at Nicaea. They merely recognized what many believers before them already understood.

My point here is twofold: there are good answers, and many of them are accessible to any who are interested to do a bit of investigating.

One other strategy that offers immense benefit when learning about a subject is taking a look at the big picture. Many Christians who have heard good Bible instruction for many years are still unclear on what the differences are between preexilic, exilic, and postexilic prophets. Getting the big picture clear helps us better make sense of all the details.

Consider the following story: I got my first computer in the 1980s, and I enlisted a savvy doctoral student at Stanford named Kent as my tutor. I told Kent to assume I knew nothing about computers, which was not entirely true—I did know that the keypad was identical to that of a typewriter. I also knew the difference between software and hardware, but I wanted Kent to start at the most basic level. Getting the big picture in any area of knowledge (and this certainly applies to history) is a strategy worth implementing.

I think the lack of interest in learning is due to a few main reasons. The first would be the anti-intellectual approach that we sketched earlier. The second one is perhaps a bigger culprit but ironically not talked about much. It is that many Christians do not put themselves in faith-stretching situations where they need to be ready to offer intelligent answers to non-Christians. The polls on Christians who share their faith confirm my own conversations. Christians do not share their faith much with neighbors, coworkers, or at the gym. In fact, many do not look for those opportunities. I've snooped around quite a bit and asked a lot of questions about this. Even in ministries that historically have been committed to sharing the gospel, you will find a precipitous drop in evangelism. If you are engaging non-Christians, the question of why we Christians privilege the Bible as God's Word will inevitably come up. I know it has for me and several friends who also talk about their faith with non-Christians. Putting yourself out there as a witness is a wonderful motivator to learn. Not putting yourself in places where all kinds of questions may be posed leaves one with much less motivation to learn.

In these sorts of discussions, it is not difficult to see that a critical practice is the desire to remember what is worth remembering while steering clear of what is not worth remembering.[39] Christians who know all about the starting lineup for the 1969 New York Mets but are woefully ignorant of history need to take stock of their priorities.

Ask God to increase your curiosity about him and the world he has created. You are hardwired to be curious about God and his world. Don't let lesser pursuits suck that desire out of you. The lack of curiosity among many Christians is one of the things that brings me great sadness. As children, we were constantly trying to figure things out. We freely asked our parents why and how things worked the way they did. This kind of inquisitiveness gets drained out of many adults by the cares of everyday life. It need not be this way. Take time to pay attention. Observe what is going on. It is easy to be distracted and not take in what is right in front of us. Consider reading a book that stretches you to think in new ways. Too many of us, to use Daniel Boorstin's illuminating term, are "aliterates." We know how to read, but we don't.[40] Those who don't read but can are in the same situation as those who can't read. It should humble "aliterates" to remember that those struggling with illiteracy are usually very eager to rectify that deficit.

Recent history can also rebuke our apathy about reading. During the late nineteenth century and into the twentieth, there was a popular program for self-education in Britain where blue-collar workers devoured classical works of literature.[41] Many of us literate and college-educated Christians need to awaken our dormant curiosity. We should take an honest inventory of why we are apathetic to learn.

Go outside, slow down, take a walk, and pay attention. What you observe will help you better understand the world that, again, is firmly grounded in history. Everything from your hometown, however big or small, has a history worth knowing. Develop a park ranger's love for knowing the land you live in.

There are huge benefits one derives from being a lifelong learner—the topic we now turn to address. The following is a sampling, but it should provide plenty of motivation.

Learning Is "Spiritual" in Nature

When I ask Christians whether prayer, reading the Bible, fellowship, worship, or giving are "spiritual" in nature, they respond with a hearty amen. When I ask most Christians whether being stretched intellectually is a spiritual matter of critical importance, most respond with something like, "I'm not a teacher, Dave. That is not my gift. Reading lots of books, especially demanding ones that stretch the mind, is not important for my spiritual development. Besides, I never was a good student." These objections seem reasonable, and many Christians hold them, but they sorely miss some critical truths.

To begin with, it is crucial to appreciate the distinction between intelligence and being an intellectual. The former refers to whatever mental aptitude God has given you;[42] the latter refers to how much you use what God has given you. It is clear, then, why well-informed people may not have as much native intelligence, while those with a higher IQ may be quite ignorant about any number of important issues.[43] I recall listening to an interview with a brilliant brain surgeon. She sheepishly admitted to not having time to read outside her own, narrow field. When asked who the vice president was at the time, she confessed to not being sure. She was finally able to dig out Dick Cheney, but it took a bit of effort. Another example was a classmate of mine at Dallas Theological Seminary. He was clearly a brilliant guy, but he struggled daily with watching too much television. He did not get good grades because he was a poor steward of the mind God had given him. As a result, he was intelligent but not a true intellectual. Pause here for a moment. Being an "intellectual" is widely viewed as synonymous with being intelligent. Unfortunately, this common conflation of words is erroneous.

To further shock the sensibilities of many, let me state that all Christians *in one sense* ought to be intellectuals. I happen to believe that *intellectual* is a word worth recovering. All

Christians, regardless of native intelligence and vocation, are called to use whatever brains God has given them. We tend to think of intellectuals in a narrower sense because there are those who spend much of their day in deep thought. We call some of these people, who regularly comment in various forms of media, "public intellectuals." It is not wholly inaccurate that we think of intellectuals in this narrow sense, but there is a broader sense that *intellectual* needs to be a descriptor for all Christians. The sage counsel of Frank Gaebelein offers some needed light: "The Christian call to the intellectual life is not just to an elite, a chosen few. We are not responsible for the extent of our native intelligence but for the extent of our use of the ability God has given us." Gaebelein proceeds to quote Professor Jacques Barzun of Columbia, who underscored the "crucial difference between intelligence and intellectualism." Intelligence is "our native endowment in mental aptitude." Intellectualism "is the use we make of our individual ability."[44]

Gaining knowledge of God and his world should not be limited to the brightest or most gifted at teaching. Scriptures like Psalms 1 and 119 make it clear that everyone's spiritual health is directly affected by personal interaction with the Word of God. Passages like Psalm 111 encourage us to become familiar with what God has been doing throughout the ages, thus underscoring the importance of a growing historical sense. One commentator rightly captures the spirit: "Psalm 111 is a hymn of praise of God's involvement in history."[45] Proverbs 6:6–8 and 30:24–31 are great reminders that there is much to learn from the physical world. You must go outside to "observe the ant." Ants are not found in your Bible—unless you have been leaving it by the food at a picnic. In other words, the Bible itself says that it is not the only important thing to know. Just reading your Bible is not the only valuable thing for your growth in godliness. Howard Hendricks, a longtime and beloved professor at Dallas Theological Seminary, liked to say while holding his Bible, "If this is the only book you ever know, you will never know this book."

Let me draw out a few implications from what Hendricks was addressing. Since the Bible speaks of real places like Babylon and real groups of people like the Sadducees, it is impossible to know the Bible well apart from the study of history. To draw out responsible theological concepts, one is helped by at least some rudimentary understanding of philosophy. Learning about the difference between *being* and *person* is helpful for making the right distinctions about the Trinity. Responsibly reading the different genres in Scripture can certainly be aided by a growing familiarity with great literature. In fact, I recently interviewed a scholar who believes the study of rhetoric should take place in every local church. It may sound ludicrous, but he made a compelling case about how the study of rhetoric could help all Christians in very practical ways.[46]

For the Christian, learning is meant to be spiritually beneficial. Though most will understand what I mean by "spiritually beneficial," I agree with Eugene Peterson that "spiritual" is not the best word to use. What's not spiritual? All of life is affected by what we are learning. And what we learn has a direct bearing on what we believe, which of course, in turn, impacts *every area* of our life.

While serving as a pastor, I vividly recall one woman who wanted to bend my ear about her husband's newfound desire to study more deeply. He wanted to wrestle more honestly with what he believed. His wife was not happy and conveyed her dismay to me in no uncertain language. It frustrated her how much her husband was wrestling through issues like the age of the earth and whether God used evolution in any significant way. Months after my first encounter with this woman, she called to confess something to me. She first asked if I remembered our conversation. It was hard to forget, so yes, I remembered it quite well. She went on to say that her husband's desire to dig deeper into his Christian faith made her uneasy with how little she knew. Her candor and humility in acknowledging this was refreshing. Tragically, she is not alone. A brilliant early nineteenth-century American writer, Alexis de Tocqueville, observed most people "either believe things without knowing why, or not know what it is they ought to believe."[47]

I am happy to report that this woman became convinced that a systematic study of the Christian faith was also of enormous benefit to her own growth as a Christian. In a later conversation, she mentioned that her marriage was also strengthened by her willingness to study with her husband.

We desperately need to advocate for communities where Christians are encouraged to learn. The Christian tradition has a rich history of being a learning community. Pursuing lifelong learning puts us squarely in the mainstream of what the Christian faith has been about since its inception. Why forfeit rich opportunities to learn from godly men and women who have much to teach us? Why forfeit rich opportunities to grow in wisdom by not increasing one's familiarity with key events and movements of the past?

If we are not being stretched intellectually at church, along with availing ourselves of other opportunities to learn, we are then in danger of holding on to whatever conceptions we have of God, whether these be true or not. In this regard, we need to heed the Bible's many warnings about idolatry. These warnings do not just refer to those outside the Christian faith. There are sober warnings about idolatry to those of us who claim Christ. For example, it is arresting to see that John closes a letter written to Christians with a warning about idolatry: "Little children, guard yourselves from idols" (1 John 5:21 NASB).

Living the Christian faith in any era is challenging. From my own study over many years, I would not want to live in any other time. When I read about how certain illnesses were treated in previous eras, I shudder. Along with the marvels of modern medicine, I am also glad for things like flushing toilets, running water, air conditioning, and so much more. These blessings, however, do not mean that we modern folk are devoid of some formidable, even unique challenges. Our own modern era clearly has some unique challenges, like our ever-growing technologies (in speed and variety), easy access to all kinds of entertainment, ridiculous ways we deny our mortality, and the incessant appeal to be consumers instead of taking time to think more thoughtfully about life. In light of these, and many other challenges, it is prudent to avail ourselves of any aids that can offer perspective. Lifelong learning of history in community, fueled by a genuine love for God and others, is a powerful prophylactic to being swept away by the cultural currents of the day.

There is much suffering in this world that can't be avoided. Then there is the suffering that can be prevented by growing in our ability to think historically. We may not be able to avoid the growing hostility toward the Christian faith, but history gives us ample insight into how others were able to live in perilous times. Instead of this, I see many Christians walking around with a debilitating lack of direction. And it never surprises me that those I see in this state of mind are not interested learners of history.

Learning Never Ends

It is a popular belief that learning eventually slows down or even stops in heaven. This is sadly one reason why too many Christians think heaven is not that compelling. I have had many conversations with Christians who admitted this to me. Too many erroneously believe that after every difficult question we have is satisfactorily answered, and we get to know every person there, heaven will begin to get a bit boring. Nothing could be further from the truth! This confuses how being without sin and having perfect bodies that will live eternally does not mean we somehow become infinite. *We remain finite in heaven.*

Our ultimate hope, which is finally realized in a perfect, glorified body and being released from sin, is something that certainly spurs us on in this life (Rom. 8:18). But we must not miss that our future glorified selves remain finite. And a finite being can never exhaust or get to the end of an infinite one—namely God. God will reveal more of himself to us throughout eternity (1 Cor. 2:9; Eph. 2:7). It is impossible to exhaust that which is, by definition, inexhaustible. Think about the implications of this when it comes to learning. Since heaven is going to be a place of perpetual learning, why not start being an avid learner now?

C. S. Lewis mentioned the need to discern between the things of childhood that ought to be discarded and those of childhood that we are unwise to discard.[48] The former includes things like being fickle, ignorant, jealous, boastful, and cruel. One of the major ones that we are unwise to discard is our curiosity. It is tragic to see many adults no longer curious to learn. Outgrowing childhood curiosity may be common among adults, but that certainly does not mean it is wise. We were created to know God, his world, others, and even ourselves. Healthy people have a bias that there is much they do not know and have not experienced. They are eager to keep growing. This is a process that will never cease.

Again, we fail to appreciate our finitude in relation to the infinite nature of God. Here we regularly commit an error. Theologian David Bentley Hart reminds us that "[God] is not the high who stands over the low, but is the infinite act of distance that gives high and low a place."[49] Our temptation to compare our smallness to God's immensity is fraught with problems from the beginning. God being infinite is a unique reality that has no comparisons. The common analogy of us being like ants and God being so much greater is not an accurate way to think about the One who called everything into existence by his limitless power. God and human beings are not on the same spectrum where we contrast finitude with infinitude. No one shares the spectrum with God!

Learning Is "Practical"

Another common error is to make a large separation between wisdom and knowledge. Like the arbitrary separation of "head and heart," we can easily separate what God has joined together. Wisdom and knowledge are distinct, to be sure, but have a much closer relationship than most Christians realize.[50] Among other things, it is the extreme separation of these two related concepts that has contributed to the problem of anti-intellectualism among Christians. For example, too many Christians believe going deeper in their knowledge is impractical and therefore a waste of time.

There is further confusion on this issue because of a widely misunderstood passage of Scripture. In 1 Corinthians 8:1, Paul says, "Knowledge puffs up, but love edifies" (NKJV). The conclusion many make is to steer clear from gaining too much knowledge, for it will make you arrogant. Love is where it is at. The first commandment after all is to love God, not know about him. There are many problems with this line of thinking. Let me briefly sketch out a few.

The context of 1 Corinthians 8:1 addresses those who feel they have the freedom to eat food sacrificed to idols and those who don't. Paul warns against allowing "this 'knowledge'" (as the ESV helpfully renders it), which gives some the freedom to eat the food, to guard against being critical of those who don't feel they have the same freedom. *It is knowledge misused, not knowledge in and of itself, that Paul is warning about.* Furthermore, we know that Paul makes many appeals to knowledge and right thinking throughout his teaching on Christian growth, so knowledge per se can't be in Paul's spiritual crosshairs.

It would make no sense for the apostle Paul to diminish the importance of knowledge when he warns against thinking like children and the need to be mature in our thinking. And this occurs in the same book as the misapplied verse of 1 Corinthians 8:1 (see 1 Cor. 14:20 NASB). Our real nemesis is pride, *not* knowledge. Pride can tempt those who know a lot, but pride can equally tempt those who may not know as much but are prideful about how zealous they are. I have been in ministry among many who were anything but modest about the radical risks they were willing to take for Jesus. I regularly heard that we were the "green berets" of Christianity. As such, we should be willing to "charge hell with a squirt gun." Even as a young believer, I remember thinking about how unwise it would be to do this. If I am going deep into the enemy's territory, it seemed wise to go with as many weapons as I could find.

As mentioned earlier, I do not particularly like using the word "spiritual." I am also leery of using the word "practical." It gives the idea, as Ken Myers of Mars Hill Audio highlighted, that something is "readily achievable"—in other words, something that is easy and requires little effort. I am certainly not advocating that popular notion of "practical," as most of this book and the next section on the painful aspect of learning make clear. Remembering this clarification, the close tie between knowledge and wisdom is practical in that the greatest benefits come from its partnership.

In Proverbs, we find such a close relationship between wisdom and knowledge. Right out of the gate in Proverbs (1:1–9), we see this symbiotic relationship. Knowledge is clearly more integral to wisdom than many of us have been led to believe. I asked biblical scholar Dru Johnson about this during my interview with him on his book *Biblical Knowing*:

> **Moore:** Many Christians make a radical distinction between knowledge and wisdom. Knowledge is what we cognitively understand, while wisdom is what we "do." Interestingly, the book of Proverbs puts knowledge and wisdom in closer proximity. We are told

that the wise person will "increase in learning" (Prov. 1:5 NASB). It seems quite clear there is a limitation to how much we can do if our knowledge base is neglected. Speak to this important synergy of wisdom and knowledge.

Johnson: Basically, Scripture sometimes conflates the terms *knowing* and *wisdom*, and at other times they seem to be on a continuum. Either way, I believe the old construct that I learned in the church—"Knowledge is knowing what's true, but wisdom is knowing what to do."—is incorrect. Wisdom is not applying knowledge content to a real-world problem. Wisdom, as developed in all of Scripture, is a skilled discernment that sees beyond the superficial circumstances. It is a transcendent vision, like the police officer who "knows" when someone is lying or a counselor who can see abuse patterns in a person's past experience.[51]

It is understandable why many of us prioritize wisdom or "living well" and diminish the importance of knowing things.[52] What many of us fail to remember is that our ability to make wise choices is limited or expanded by what we know. Knowledge alone does not guarantee we will choose wisely, but increasing knowledge makes it easier to determine the wisest course of action. It is also why the wise person in Proverbs is instructed to seek out godly counsel. No one knows it all, so it is crucial to avail oneself of godly people who have insight we don't possess.

Norm Abram is known as the host of two PBS shows: *This Old House* and *The New Yankee Workshop*. He is a true master carpenter with an amazing knowledge about all aspects of working with wood. His vast learning does not magically guarantee he will choose his materials wisely and make great furniture. After all, it is possible to conceive of skilled people who are unscrupulous and cut corners. Norm is not one of them. His beautiful craftsmanship speaks volumes for the "practicality" of his sophisticated knowledge of carpentry.

Now consider the other side of things. You can have a carpenter who has impeccable ethics, is conscientious to a fault, and desperately wants to make great furniture. His problem in carrying out these noble pursuits resides not in his desire but in his lack of knowledge about woodworking. He has not put in the proper amount of effort to learn his craft. His heart may be in the right place, but his knowledge is too superficial. His lack of knowledge results in all kinds of problems. Among other things, he will not be able to make a decent living as a carpenter.

Again, knowledge alone does not guarantee wise living, but expanding our knowledge does provide the means whereby we can make more prudent decisions. A personal example should shed some further light. Let's say my car's transmission is on its last legs. As a point of fact, I don't happen to know much about cars. I have learned some things over the years, but my knowledge about the proper functioning of a car engine is limited. I do want to be a wise steward of my financial resources, but the ability to do so in this case is held hostage by my ignorance of cars. Will the mechanic try to take advantage of my ignorance? I don't have the knowledge to be able to determine whether that will be the case. As a result, I am not always sure of what the wisest course of action is. My lack of knowledge about cars highlights yet again how we suffer for our ignorance.

One popular writer of American history, Joy Hakim, bemoans our society's de-emphasis on teaching great ideas to children. Hakim also notes that too many teachers spend inordinate time on methodology and fail to develop adequate proficiency in the subject they are teaching.[53] This is a major crisis in education. If the teacher doesn't care to know the subject—well, guess what the outcome will be for the students? And this kind of apathetic approach occurs at all levels of education. One university professor told me that some of his colleagues kept regurgitating the same lecture notes year after year. If the notes were good enough (and they weren't) thirty years ago, why not keep using them? Intellectual laziness can be found in all sorts of places—even some that we might not typically consider.

Helping others grow in their *knowledge* of the influential movements, ideas, and people of the past offers much *potential wisdom* for everyday living. Again, it does not guarantee that expanding one's knowledge will yield greater wisdom. It does guarantee that the capacity to make wise decisions will broaden for those who gain knowledge properly. Learning with this sort of posture is an exceedingly important *and* practical matter. The wildly popular biographer David McCullough discusses this in his characteristically incisive way:

> Knowing about a subject is important because you want to know what you're talking about when you're teaching. But beyond that, you can't love what you don't know. And the great teachers—the teachers who influence you, who change your lives—almost always, I'm sure, are the teachers that love what they

> are teaching. It is that wonderful teacher who says, "Come over here and look in this microscope, you're really going to get a kick out of this."[54]

As noted earlier, there is no doubt that *proper* learning will also expand one's ability to minister to a wider array of people and at a deeper level. Too many Christians who desire to impact others seem to be unaware, or need to be reminded regularly, of this benefit.

Learning Is Painful

It is painful to find out that a belief you thought to be true has been proven to be incorrect. Perhaps this is the biggest reason why many of us steer clear of lifelong learning. Things like laziness and not knowing where to start are typically listed as the biggest impediments to learning, but I'm convinced that the fear of being proven wrong may be an even bigger reason for not wanting to learn. Deciding to be a lifelong learner means we are willing to put ourselves in a place of vulnerability. We've determined that submitting our beliefs to scrutiny is worth the embarrassment of being proven wrong. Sadly, many of us find it too threatening to place ourselves in such a posture. One scholar does a good job of laying out the risks inherent in learning:

> The ancient Greeks saw it as axiomatic that to learn was to suffer, and they reduced that conviction to a maxim: *mathein pathein.* Why that connection? *Learning* demands *suffering* because it is painful to open the mind and the heart to new truth. Pain is the symptom of a system in disequilibrium. . . . Pain

> likewise results from the need to stretch mental muscles around new ways of viewing the world.[55]

In his seminal book on Christian education, John Hull has an entire chapter devoted to "The Need to be Right and the Pain of Learning."[56] We ought to put a premium on thinking more carefully about why we think in the ways we do. Unfortunately, most of us find this too costly. Ironically, the greater cost comes from not thinking about such things. As we have already underscored, what we don't know really can hurt us.

Walt Henrichsen, author of the best-selling *Disciples Are Made Not Born*, liked to say that "all good discipleship means the undoing of some bad discipleship." In other words, many of us have been taught things by well-intentioned people, but that does not mean these things are correct. Walt once told a few of us that he was like "a garlic milkshake" to many people. His probing questions and wide-ranging learning were simply too much for the masses. Original and thoughtful thinkers like Walt should be valued. Too bad most of us don't have the stomach for such a challenge.

I often use the illustration here of a brick as representing an erroneous idea we hold on some important subject. If we do not allow our "bricks" to be inspected by wise people, it is easy to start erecting a wall. It seems like the natural thing to do. A wall of this sort, however, is much more intimidating to face than a few bricks. I think of the delightful eighty-five-year-old man who spent a year in the church history class I was teaching. This octogenarian was convinced about his interpretation of end-time matters, or what theologians call *eschatology*. His strong convictions carried a lot of credibility. Since he had studied the Bible for most of his long life, it made sense to him (and others) that he must be right. In my class, I raised some concerns about the history surrounding his cherished view. My material was prepared beforehand, so I had no idea how important this issue would be to anyone in the class. As you can imagine, my teaching brought some pain to this elderly brother. Fortunately, we had a strong enough relationship to talk through why I was teaching what I was teaching. My friend never altered his view. I can report that he did start to hold his position a bit more tentatively in light of what he learned in the class.

I've had many experiences where it became clear that my belief on some matter must be wrong. Even some of my cherished beliefs have been upended. Allow me to provide a few of these. For example, I attended Dallas Theological Seminary (DTS) in the early 1980s. I am deeply grateful for the education and the relationships I made during my time there. During my studies at DTS, I heard the following from various professors: "If you give up the belief that the original documents of the Bible are without error (commonly called the inerrancy of Scripture), you will be led inexorably to a more *liberal* view of the Bible. You may even abandon the orthodox Christian faith altogether." Some examples of individuals who followed this path were mentioned to make the case sound persuasive. At the time, I was only a young Christian, and my professors were much more learned than I. What my professors said seemed to make sense. Fast-forward a bit—about a decade after graduating from seminary, I got to know a professor of Old Testament studies from another seminary. He didn't quite subscribe to the doctrine of inerrancy, yet he was hardly a theological liberal. He was rock solid on the important teachings of the Christian faith, along with being courageous in his understanding of Scripture on controversial topics like sexual ethics. In fact, he was one of the lone voices in his decidedly more liberal seminary. I was baffled. This man lives under the authority of Scripture in ways that would impress any person who holds to the inerrancy of God's word. What to do? Well, I altered my view. My view of inerrancy did not dramatically change, but I did change my view about some who do not believe in the inerrancy of Scripture. It may be the case that *some* go off the theological rails by abandoning the inerrancy of Scripture. It is clearly not the case that abandoning inerrancy is a "watershed" (a word I heard often from my professors) that logically leads to theological liberalism.

Here's another example: For many years, I heard that love had nothing to do with feelings. It made sense since "everyone knows" our feelings are fickle while love is to be constant. I heard this from all kinds of people. I certainly heard it from passionate preachers on marriage. "Don't worry," they would tell us, "if your feelings fluctuate for your spouse. Love is a commitment. Feelings are not particularly important. Feelings come and go." I agree that love is a commitment since it is a covenant we make before God and others. But are feelings as unimportant as many believe? My view on this was challenged from a fresh interaction with the very text used to prove that feelings are unimportant. I am speaking of Ephesians 5. It is common to hear the argument for the unimportance of feelings in a sort of logical syllogism based on this section of Scripture. It goes like this: Paul commands husbands to love their wives as Christ loves the church (v. 25). Then we are told that you can't command someone's feelings. Therefore, love does not involve feelings. It seems like a pretty solid line of reasoning. The problem is that two of the following verses in Ephesians 5 undermine such logic. Verses 28 and 29 say, "So husbands also ought to love their own wives as their own bodies. He who loves his own wife loves himself; for no one ever hated his own flesh, but nourishes and cherishes it, just as Christ also *does* the church" (NASB). To catch the weight of what is being said here, let me offer an illustration. Let's say a husband comes home to tell his wife that the promotion rightly due him was given to another person who is less qualified. How do you picture him telling his wife? Is he robotic, devoid of emotion? Hardly. We imagine him showing all kinds of emotion as he voices his frustration over the injustice. He is quite committed to his own well-being. To use Paul's language, he "nourishes and cherishes" himself. All his being is involved in his care for himself, which is the precise way he is instructed to care for his wife. So, love without feeling is hardly love. Yes, there may be times when these feelings are not as strong, but we should not give ourselves a pass when our love consistently does not involve feelings. Realizing how many were committing the error of saying "love has nothing to do with feelings" made me wonder how many other things I believed to be true from well-intentioned speakers and writers on marriage.

The apostle Paul offers further help in this regard. We find it in the "love chapter" of the Bible, 1 Corinthians 13. Consider verse 3: "And if I give all my possessions to feed the poor, and if I surrender my body to be burned, but do not have love, it profits me nothing" (NASB). Giving up all one's possessions is impressive. Having your body burned is the ultimate in self-sacrifice. Both these actions are remarkable, but note well that you can do both without a scrap of love. Yes, love shows itself in various actions or obedience to God's commands, but love involves more than just performing some duty.[57]

True learning involves pain, but if we desire to know the truth, the only wise option is to dig in deeply and constantly put ourselves in a place where we may be proven wrong.

Learning Is Serious Business, but That's Not the Whole Story

Jewish rabbis believe that one of the first questions asked during the judgment to come is whether one set aside "regular periods to study the Torah."[58] Jews also believe that learning is incumbent upon everyone, not just a select few.[59] Adam Marlin is a recent convert to the Jewish faith who earned three Ivy League degrees. He was greatly impressed by those who had been studying the Talmud for many years yet came from "small religious schools." Marlin confessed that they were able to "dance intellectual circles" around him.[60]

Think about it this way. We are aware of what we know, we are aware of some things we don't know, but what can really hurt us are the things we aren't aware of not knowing. Being ignorant of our ignorance in certain areas can be lethal, and sincerity offers no protection. The well-known illustration of the guy who doesn't appreciate gravity and feels he can leap from a tall building without any serious repercussions makes a self-evident and sobering point.

Learning is serious business,[61] but it would be wrong to conclude that it must be pure drudgery. Learning should involve delight, even joy. Cotton Mather described how the pupils under the care of Ezekiel Cheever, the highly regarded schoolmaster of the Massachusetts Bay Colony, "came to work as though they came to play."[62] David McCullough adds that history (and studying other subjects as well) gives pleasure because it offers an "expansion of the experience of being alive."[63] Recall what Daniel Levitin said at the beginning of this book. We are hardwired to make sense of our world, and this brings deep delight.

Benefits to You and Your Ministry

An interesting diagnostic set of questions I have offered to various groups revolves around the two commandments of Jesus in Matthew 10:16, where we are to be "shrewd as serpents and innocent as doves." Before I ask my questions, I make sure that everyone understands that Jesus is obviously using "shrewd" in a positive way. Though we might think of shrewd people as cunning or unprincipled, Jesus is talking about being the kind of person who has a godly sense of discernment. We might call it "spiritual street smarts." I proceed by asking how many know someone who has this kind of shrewdness. Several hands go up. I then ask the group if they know anyone who could be characterized as "innocent as a dove." Again, several hands go up. My last question, and the one I am most curious about, is this: How many of you know someone who has both a godly shrewdness *and* is innocent as a dove? No kidding, I am still waiting for someone to raise their hand. Embodying both "shrewd as a serpent and innocent as a dove" is a supernatural feat, but the two are both important to Jesus.

Learning can help us grow in both shrewdness and innocence. And growing in our understanding of history, and how responsible history is written, offers great benefits here. Learning is not magical in this regard. Many times, learning seems to lead people to be cunning and corrupt, but if we submit to learning the way Jesus commands, we can find the motivation to be increasingly marked as both shrewd and pure of heart. Our world desperately needs people who model both these qualities in godly tension with one another.

Some Thoughts on Engagement with the Rest of the Book

Make sure to jot down your reflections and questions as you make your way through the rest of this book. You will discover new implications and applications for your life as you work through this material. Capturing your thoughts with an ever-ready writing instrument adds immeasurable benefit to your study. As the old adage goes, "The palest ink is more retentive than the best memory." Writing down notes and underlining keeps us engaged. John Adams sometimes would write so feverishly on what he was reading that it seemed his own writing exceeded that of the book itself. In one book, the marginal notes made by Adams came to 12,000 words![64] Now *that* is active engagement with reading. Research shows that memory is better aided when we write things down in the old analog sort of way. Typing does not have the same impact.[65] I would like to ban all computers in academic settings, except for those who may need them if they truly help with things like dysgraphia. Most of us would be better off sticking to pen and paper.

At one church where I taught this material, people regularly thanked me for being so open to interacting over any and all issues. My own struggles to make sense of the Christian faith compel me to be vigilant about stimulating discussion on the topics that truly matter. We should not be intimidated by the hard questions. When we cordon off some issues or give them a religious taboo status, we undermine the whole educational process. The disciplined study of history reminds us that all sorts of people wrestled with the very things that trouble us today. The packaging of these problems may look different (cars instead of chariots), but the root causes are similar. Money, sex, and power have animated people throughout human history.

Timothy Larsen writes of ministers in Victorian England who *deconverted* from Christianity due to an ongoing "crisis of doubt."[66] These struggling ministers were sometimes told by terribly misguided Christians to stay away from reading the writings of skeptics. The recommendation was to have a simple trust in Jesus and not bother with thornier intellectual issues. This counsel hardly kept all the thoughtful ministers in Victorian England from deconverting. Fortunately, many of those ministers who deconverted due to nagging doubts later came back to the Christian faith. They *reconverted* when they saw for themselves that the biblical account of reality seemed more credible than the one trumpeted by critics of the Bible.

One of my favorite writers on education and culture, the late Neil Postman, believed the most important educational skill was asking good questions.[67] He was incredulous that teachers no longer taught students how to ask good questions.

In his characteristically humorous and incisive way, Postman had a strong hunch about why this was the case:

> What will happen if a student, studying history, asks, "Whose history is this?" What will happen if a student, having been given a definition (of anything) asks, "Who made up this definition? Are there other ways to define this thing?" What will happen if a student, being given a set of facts, asks, "What is a fact? How is it different from an opinion? And who is the judge?"[68]

Postman's observation also raises the concerns articulated earlier by Joy Hakim and David McCullough. It seems likely that some teachers don't give instruction in asking good questions because of their own insecurity about how well they have studied their subject. Our master carpenter, Norm Abram, would not be intimidated to answer any and all questions about working with wood. And he is wise enough to know how much there still is for him to learn. If you have watched either one of his shows, you see Norm constantly asking other experts why and how they work in the ways they do. In other words, Norm is secure enough in his considerable knowledge to admit when he doesn't know something.

No one should feel uncomfortable asking difficult questions. We sin against our brothers and sisters in Christ when we make them feel less "spiritual" for raising challenging questions about important matters.

Note you will find discussion questions at the end of each chapter. I have tried to provide probing and provocative questions to stimulate a thoughtful engagement with the material. You are reading the result of many years of reading, reflection, teaching, and certainly struggle. I count it a great honor to have the opportunity to publish the fruit of this work.

Discussion Questions

1. What are some other principles of learning, aside from those presented in this chapter?

2. Give some examples from Scripture where learning is understood as indispensable for the growing Christian.

3. Is television your major impediment to learning? If not, are there any hobbies that may be consuming too much of your time, thereby limiting the learning process?

4. Isn't it interesting how many Christians get lost in singing songs with words like "hallelujah" or "hosanna" (not to mention "raising one's Ebenezer"), yet do not know what they mean?[69] What are some ideas that could help leaders better instruct the congregation in meaningful worship?

Getting lost in the beauty of the music while failing to consider the content is nothing new. Augustine mentions how it was a constant temptation for him to love music and not pay attention to the truth being conveyed. Unlike some Christians, Augustine did not think the answer was found in getting rid of music altogether but in remembering to focus on the words being sung. And yet Augustine remained vigilant in guarding against the temptation to get lost in the seductive nature of music. Discuss the following reflection of Augustine: "Yet when it happens to me that the music moves me more than the subject of the song, I confess myself to commit a sin deserving punishment, and then I would prefer not to have heard the singer."[70]

NOTES

[1]See Nathan O. Hatch, *The Democratization of American Christianity* (New Haven, CT: Yale University Press, 1989).

[2]Daniel J. Levitin, *The Organized Mind: Thinking Straight in an Age of Information Overload* (New York: Dutton, 2014), 32; emphasis added.

[3]For a terrific example of Augustine's relevance, see James K. A. Smith, *On the Road with Saint Augustine* (Grand Rapids: Brazos Press, 2019).

[4]Donald Kagan, "In Defense of History" (34th Jefferson Lecture in the Humanities, Washington, DC, May 12, 2005), 10. This incisive address is posted at www.neh.gov/whoweare/kagan/lecture.html. Also see page 11. Other historians make the same distinction between being a historian and being a chronicler. See John Warwick Montgomery, *Where Is History Going?* (Minneapolis: Bethany Fellowship, 1969), 79; Ronald H. Nash, *Christian Faith and Historical Understanding* (Grand Rapids: Zondervan, 1984), 13–14; and Jonathan T. Pennington, *Reading the Gospels Wisely: A Narrative and Theological Introduction* (Grand Rapids: Baker Academic, 2012), 95.

[5]See David George Moore, "Interview with Wilfred McClay on *Land of Hope*," *Patheos/Jesus Creed* (blog), October 5, 2019.

[6]This does not eliminate the possibility that the historical record may need some correction or revision. For example, the standard number of those killed during the Civil War stood at 620,000 for many years. The

number has now been revised to around 750,000. See Guy Gugliotta, "New Estimate Raises Civil War Death Toll," *New York Times*, April 2, 2012. Regardless of the number (and it is good to have a more accurate accounting), there is much we can know about the casualties of the war.

[7] I am happy to say that I know many in all three of these arenas who greatly value education. They are a great encouragement, but they are in the minority.

[8] For a discussion of some of the shortcomings of the Puritans, see Leland Ryken, "Learning from Negative Example: Some Puritan Faults," chap. 11 in *Worldly Saints: The Puritans as They Really Were* (Grand Rapids: Zondervan, 1986).

[9] Richard Hofstadter, *Anti-intellectualism in American Life* (New York: Vintage Books, 1962), 86.

[10] For a revealing look at this particular "doctoral" degree, see David F. Wells, "The D-Min-ization of the Ministry," in *No God, But God*, ed. Os Guinness and John Seel (Grand Rapids: Baker Books, 1992), 175–88. Also see David F. Wells, *No Place for Truth, or Whatever Happened to Evangelical Theology?* (Grand Rapids: William B. Eerdmans, 1993), 218–57, esp. 235–36.

[11] See Merold Westphal, *Suspicion and Faith: The Modern Uses of Atheism* (New York: Fordham University Press, 1998). A short article that provides a good overview can be found online: see Merold Westphal, "Atheism for Lent," *The Other Side* 11 (February 20, 2008).

[12] I've written a few pieces on Emerson: David George Moore, "Where's Waldo?," *The Gospel Coalition*, March 27, 2017; and "Where's Waldo?," *Knowing & Doing*, C. S. Lewis Institute, Fall 2017.

[13] James Davison Hunter has noticed the same thing. See his *American Evangelicalism: Conservative Religion and the Quandary of Modernity* (New Brunswick, NJ: Rutgers University Press, 1983), 93–96.

[14] As quoted in Hofstadter, *Anti-intellectualism*, 87. I am well aware of the concerns over aspects of Hofstadter's thesis. I follow David Wells, Mark Noll, Os Guinness, et al. in citing *certain* features of Hofstadter's work that still have merit.

[15] See Harry S. Stout, "The Puritans behind the Myths," *Christian History* 41 (n.d.): 43.

[16] J. I. Packer, *A Quest for Godliness* (Wheaton, IL: Crossway Books, 1990), 15. Also see Ryken, *Worldly Saints*, 159.

[17] I highly recommend Gary Parrett and J. I. Packer, *Grounded in the Gospel: Building Believers the Old-Fashioned Way* (Grand Rapids: Baker Books, 2010), and Gerald L. Sittser, *Resilient Faith: How the Early Christian "Third Way" Saved the World* (Grand Rapids: Brazos Press, 2019). I am glad to know some churches where serious and long-term theological training takes place while always keeping in mind the importance of Christian formation.

[18] Frank Gaebelein, *The Christian, The Arts, and Truth* (Portland: Multnomah Press, 1985), 118.

[19] Smith, *On the Road with Saint Augustine*, 143–44; emphasis in original.

[20] As quoted in Richard Baxter, *The Reformed Pastor* (Portland: Multnomah Press, 1982), 14.

[21] Dorothy L. Sayers, *Creed or Chaos?* (Manchester, NH: Sophia Institute, 1949), 19.

[22] Sayers, *Creed or Chaos?*, 19.

[23] Sayers, *Creed or Chaos?*, 20–21.

[24] See C. S. Lewis, *Surprised by Joy* (New York: Harcourt Brace & Co., 1984), 236.

[25] Lesslie Newbigin, *Proper Confidence: Faith, Doubt, and Certainty in Christian Discipleship* (Grand Rapids: William B. Eerdmans, 1995), 14–15. Also see 38–39.

[26] Jonathan Edwards, *Religious Affections* (Portland: Multnomah Press, 1984), 105. Also see Jonathan Edwards, "Christian Knowledge: Importance and Advantage of a Thorough Knowledge of Divine Truth," in *The Works of Jonathan Edwards*, vol. 2, ed. Edward Hickman (Carlisle, PA: Banner of Truth Trust, 1988), 955–60.

[27] Jeffrey D. Arthurs, *Preaching as Reminding: Stirring Memory in an Age of Forgetfulness* (Downers Grove, IL: InterVarsity Press, 2016), 57.

[28] I am grateful to David Thomsen for this reminder.

[29] Yuval Levin, *The Great Debate: Edmund Burke, Thomas Paine, and the Birth of Left and Right* (New York: Basic Books, 2014), 66.

[30] It is important to remember the difference between hard work and discipline. If you love to study, you may work hard at it, but little discipline is needed. If you would rather do other things than study, discipline is needed. So, your "effort," as mentioned previously, may involve both hard work and discipline. I am grateful to the late Dan DeHaan, who helped to clarify this issue for me.

[31] Gaebelein, *The Christian, the Arts*, 154–55.

[32] Many thanks to Joel Altsman for sending me the quotes by Marx and Frost.

[33] If you want to read about the massive influence of television on American culture, a terrific starting point is Neil Postman, *Amusing Ourselves to Death* (New York: Penguin Books, 1985). Postman does a great job of unpacking Marshall McLuhan's famous aphorism that the "medium is the message." In other words, the way you receive information affects how you understand that information. For example, the ever-changing images of television news require us to form our opinion quickly, whereas an article about the same story offers freedom to ponder it in a more thoughtful manner. I interviewed Postman on his book *Amusing Ourselves to Death* ("Moore about Faith" on KIXL radio, November 22, 1997). This

interview and many others will eventually be available free of charge on www.mooreengaging.com.

[34]Broadcast of December 18, 1993. I don't recall the particular station, but all of the major networks are guilty of doing this.

[35]National radio broadcast on CBS (January 12, 2010).

[36]Neil Postman, *Technopoly: The Surrender of Culture to Technology* (New York: Vintage Books, 1993), 56–57.

[37]Postman, *Technopoly,* 57.

[38]I would make an exception for those who have illnesses and infirmities that limit how much face-to-face interaction they can get.

[39]See the terrific book by Arthurs, *Preaching as Reminding.*

[40]I discovered this term by reading Witold Rybczynski, *Waiting for the Weekend* (New York: Penguin Books, 1991), 192.

[41]See Edith Hall, "Classics for the People," *AEON*, November 13, 2019.

[42]Debate exists as to whether IQ remains static throughout the course of one's entire life. Some argue, and I tend to believe it has merit, that intelligence can increase or decrease (to some degree), depending on how consistently one stretches one's mind.

[43]Stupidity and ignorance are distinct concepts. They may be related but need not be. See Douglas Wilson, *Recovering the Lost Tools of Learning* (Wheaton, IL: Crossway Books, 1991), 34. Failing to appreciate the difference between intelligence and knowledge can result in someone thinking they are slow intellectually when that is hardly the case. See J. D. Vance, *Hillbilly Elegy: A Memoir of a Family and Culture in Crisis* (New York: HarperCollins, 2016), 59 and 108.

[44]Gaebelein, *The Christian, the Arts,* 152. At Cornell, a major motivation for the university dropping certain core subjects was the students being "bored" by them. See Allan Bloom, *The Closing of the American Mind* (New York: Simon and Schuster, 1987), 320.

[45]Frank E. Gaebelein, ed., *The Expositor's Bible Commentary* (Grand Rapids: Zondervan, 1991), vol. 5, *Psalms,* by Willem A. Van Gemeren, 700.

[46]See David George Moore, "Interview with James Beitler," *Patheos/Jesus Creed*, July 27, 2019.

[47]As quoted in Joseph Epstein, *Alexis de Tocqueville: Democracy's Guide* (New York: Harper Collins, 2006), 201.

[48]C. S. Lewis, *An Experiment in Criticism* (Cambridge, UK: Cambridge University Press, 1996), 71–73.

[49]As quoted in Kelly M. Kapic, *A Little Book for New Theologians* (Downers Grove, IL: InterVarsity Press, 2012), 89.

[50]After a lengthy study of Proverbs, my own conclusions about this topic were confirmed by reading the work of others. For a good summary of the issue, see the brief but helpful comments of Duane A. Garrett, *The New*

American Commentary: Proverbs, Ecclesiastes, and Song of Songs (Nashville: Broadman Press, 1993), 67.

[51] See David George Moore, "Interview with Dru Johnson," *Patheos/Jesus Creed*, July 12, 2014.

[52] A brief but wise meditation on these themes can be found in John R. W. Stott, *Your Mind Matters* (Downers Grove, IL: InterVarsity Press, 1972).

[53] "In Depth with Joy Hakim," BookTV, December 6, 2009.

[54] David McCullough, "Knowing History and Knowing Who We Are," *Imprimis* (April 2005): 3.

[55] Luke Timothy Johnson, *Living Jesus: Learning the Heart of the Gospel* (San Francisco: Harper Collins, 1999), 61; emphasis in original.

[56] See John M. Hull, *What Prevents Christian Adults from Learning?* (Philadelphia: Trinity Press International), 1985.

[57] I am grateful to Jason Fikes for reminding me of this teaching in 1 Corinthians. For a terrific book on this subject, I highly recommend Matthew A. Elliott, *Faithful Feelings: Rethinking Emotion in the New Testament* (Grand Rapids: Kregel Publications, 2006).

[58] Marvin R. Wilson, *Our Father Abraham* (Grand Rapids: William B. Eerdmans, 1989), 304.

[59] Wilson, *Our Father Abraham*, 300.

[60] As quoted in Cal Newport, *Deep Work: Rules for Focused Success in a Distracted World* (New York: Grand Central, 2016), 156.

[61] One scholar registers a caution about thinking only radical ideas matter. It is easy to understand how "ideas have consequences" when they come from the likes of a Stalin or Hitler. Less radical ideas work quietly into the fabric of society but can eventually bring significant change. See the brilliant reflections of Gertrude Himmelfarb, *On Looking into the Abyss* (New York: Alfred A. Knopf, 1994), xii. Also see Stott, *Your Mind Matters*, 12–13.

[62] As quoted in Page Smith, *Killing the Spirit: Higher Education in America* (New York: Viking, 1990), 210.

[63] McCullough, "Knowing History," 4.

[64] David McCullough, *John Adams* (New York: Simon & Schuster, 2001), 619.

[65] Lizette Borreli, "Why Using Pen and Paper, Not Laptops, Boosts Memory: Writing Notes Helps Recall Concepts, Ability to Understand," *Medical Daily*, February 6, 2014.

[66] See Timothy Larsen, *Crisis of Doubt: Honest Faith in Nineteenth Century England* (Oxford: Oxford University Press, 2006).

[67] Neil Postman, *Building a Bridge to the Eighteenth Century* (New York: Alfred A. Knopf, 1999), 161.

[68] Postman, *Building a Bridge to the Eighteenth Century*, 162.

[69] This problem can become especially acute in churches that are loaded with musical talent. In such settings, it is easy to get lost in the beauty of the music and so fail to internalize the content. Pastors need to teach and encourage the body to worship in "spirit and truth" (John 4:21–24 NASB).

[70] Augustine, *Confessions*, trans. Henry Chadwick (New York: Oxford University Press, 1991), 10:33. I am grateful to my wife, Doreen, for reminding me of this section in *Confessions*.

CHAPTER TWO

WHY THE PAST IS NOT THE PAST

Not to know what took place before you were born is to remain a child forever. **—Cicero**

Tradition is the living faith of the dead while traditionalism is the dead faith of the living. **—Jaroslav Pelikan**

Trying to plan for the future without a sense of the past is like trying to plant cut flowers. **—Daniel Boorstin**

Many of us vividly recall the boring history classes we endured in school. The droning of the teacher convinced us that history's main benefit was in giving the historian something to do.

Being unimpressed with the importance of history shows up in how accurately we recall what really transpired. Richard Lederer "pasted together the following history of the world from genuine student bloopers collected by teachers throughout the United States, from eighth grade through college level."[1] There are several to pick from, but here are a few of my favorites:

> Ancient Egypt was inhabited by mummies, and they all wrote in hydraulics. They lived in the Sarah Dessert and traveled by Camelot. The climate of the Sarah is

such that the inhabitants have to live elsewhere, so certain areas of the dessert are cultivated by irritation.

Moses led the Hebrews to the Red Sea, where they made unleavened bread, which is bread made without any ingredients. Afterwards, Moses went up on Mount Cyanide to get the ten commandments. He died before he ever reached Canada.

David was a Hebrew king skilled at playing the liar. He fought with the Finkelsteins, a race of people who lived in Biblical times. Solomon, one of David's sons, had three hundred wives and seven hundred porcupines.

Socrates was a famous Greek teacher who went around giving people advice. They killed him. Socrates died from an overdose of wedlock. After his death, his career suffered a dramatic decline.

The greatest writer of the Renaissance was William Shakespeare. Shakespeare was born in the year 1564, supposedly on his birthday. He never made much money and is famous only because of his plays. He wrote tragedies, comedies, and hysterectomies, all in Islamic pentameter.

Writing at the same time as Shakespeare was Miguel Cervantes. He wrote *Donkey Hote*. The next great author was John Milton. Milton wrote *Paradise Lost*. Then his wife died and he wrote *Paradise Regained*.

Delegates from the original 13 states formed the Contented Congress. Thomas Jefferson, a Virgin, and

> Benedict Franklin were two singers of the Declaration of Independence. Franklin invented electricity by rubbing two cats backwards and declared, "A horse divided against itself cannot stand." Franklin died in 1790 and is still dead. Bach was the most famous composer in the world, and so was Handel. Handel was half German, half Italian, and half English. He was very large.

You get the idea. All kidding aside, a well-stocked and readily available memory of the past is a great aid to living wisely. Among others, it is encouraging to see a chorus of popular business gurus recognize the importance of reading history. Jim Collins considers most business books to be a waste of time and instead encourages the reading of philosophy, the arts, biography, and lots of history. According to Collins, these kinds of books give the reader "a better return on investment."[2] Tom Peters picked a history book as his "management" book of the year,[3] and Steven Sample, former president of the University of Southern California, enthusiastically underscores the indispensable nature of great books.[4] Others, like Stephen Covey, encourage the business community to be avid readers. Covey believes executives should make it a goal to read one book per week.[5]

It was a wonderful privilege to interview the late Tony Horwitz.[6] Tony received us joyfully at his wonderful place on Martha's Vineyard. Tony won the Pulitzer Prize for journalism but is best known for his popular books, like *Confederates in the Attic* and *Blue Latitudes*. Tony was a rarity: he was both thoughtful and humorous, quick with kind gestures, yet comfortable speaking his own mind.

A few years back, Tony was invited to speak on a panel at the annual meeting of the American Historical Association (AHA). He lamented that academic writing about history was far too "boring, humorless, and lacking in passion." And keep in mind that he was speaking to academics! Tony conveyed his serious concerns in a winsome manner, but that didn't reduce the pointed nature of his comments. He added that he had sat in on many of the talks at the AHA conference. Here is a bit of what he said:

> The very few papers, I'm sorry to say, that have really stood out for me have been those in which the speaker's delivery and content conveyed sincere passion. While listening to many others, I felt a bit like a marriage counselor. I wanted to shout out: "Please tell me what is it that made you fall in love with this subject in the first place, and want to live with it day and night for years! Because I'm not seeing any joy and passion."[7]

A related problem has surfaced in my various conversations with historians. Historians who ply their craft in the academic guild know that telling a good story can be frowned upon by fellow historians, especially if that work appeals to the masses. Perhaps this is changing with historians at leading universities writing responsible *and* accessible history. I am thinking, for example, of historians like Doris Kearns Goodwin, Jill Lepore, Joanne Freeman, Andrew Delbanco, David Blight, Joseph Ellis, and many more.

Why the Past Is Not Past

The title of this chapter is inspired by the famous line of the great writer William Faulkner. Lots of truth hangs on this line.

Christians should have a special interest in history. In fact, it was the historical nature of Christianity that C. S. Lewis, while still an unbeliever, found so compelling.[8] Others rightly remind us that the incarnation of Jesus underscores the prominent place of history for the Christian faith.[9] Professor Mark Noll puts the issue this way: "It is the Word of God who became flesh that encourages Bible-believing evangelicals to look seriously at the realm of the flesh." This is "the sphere of God's fullest manifestation of himself."[10] Theologian Michael Horton adds: "In biblical religion, God not only created the world (material as well as spiritual), and pronounced it 'good,' *but also created matter and history in which to unfold his salvation.*"[11]

Among other things, Jesus coming to earth demonstrates the value God places on the concrete realities of life. Events in time and space matter to Jesus, so they ought to matter to us. My double mention here of "matter" was unintended. Christians are to place a premium on material realities. We are embodied beings living in a physical reality. We present our entire bodies to God (Rom. 12:1–2). Christianity has always been at odds with the Gnostic disregard for the physical world. One of my favorite writers, Fleming Rutledge, used to have the self-descriptor of "anti-Gnostic" on her Twitter account. It is no wonder why she has so much to say about the person and work of Christ.

Advantages of Studying History

Imagine getting amnesia—no sense of who you are, your family, your friends, your job. A. W. Tozer met one such individual. In the words of Tozer, this particular young man "lost his memory and thus lost his identity." As Tozer tried to help the young man sort out his identity, someone saw them talking. The following dialogue describes the poignant scene Tozer witnessed:

> Just then I noticed a distinguished gentleman standing on the sidewalk near us. He too looked rather puzzled and uncertain, but as he glanced toward our bench, he let out a sudden, delighted shout—almost a scream. He rushed over to us and called my bewildered friend by his name. He grabbed him quickly and shook his hand. "Where have you been and what have you been doing? Everyone in the orchestra is worried sick about you." The lost man was still bewildered.
>
> "Pardon me, sir, but I do not know you. I do not recognize you."
>
> "What? You do not know me? We came to Toronto together three days ago. Don't you know that we are members of the Philharmonic and that you are the first violinist? We have filled our engagement without you and we have been searching everywhere for you!"
>
> "So that is who I am and that is why I am here! But I still don't know whether I can play a violin."[12]

Remembering the past gives perspective to the present and helps us plan wisely as we anticipate the future. Remembering important events of the past has many advantages. What follows are a few of them. Think of this as an extended section of "Benefits to You and Your Ministry." There are other things that could be mentioned, but I think this covers most of the main ones.

Detecting Blind Spots

History allows us to leave our own culture, with its set of assumptions, biases, and values. Daily we are deluged with the idea that the "latest is the greatest." We swim in this ocean. Like fish, it is hard to imagine that there is any other reality. The glories of the present and the never-ending possibilities of the future are what matters. This is why many see technological advances as unmitigated blessings. The past is rarely invoked, and when it is, it too many times becomes an illustration of how backward and misguided those people must have been.

Travel has long been regarded as integral to a complete education. Even if we don't have the time or money for physical travel, through the study of history, we can journey to distant places, both chronologically and geographically. And we can vicariously encounter what others have experienced. This is a huge help in detecting our own cultural blind spots.[13] Historian Forrest McDonald offers an arresting example:

> For instance, you don't have to rob and kill an old lady to feel the guilty torment of soul that would follow: simply read Dostoyevsky's *Crime and Punishment*. What I am saying is that a good book deals with reality in a meaningful way, by making us *feel* what is real.[14]

It was interesting to read Professor McDonald's insight, especially since my wife said her own reading *Crime and Punishment* put her in the mind of a criminal in a most vivid and sometimes sympathetic way. I am glad to report that my wife has remained a law-abiding citizen. My wife has spent time in prison—but only as a visiting Bible teacher.

Even a book about criminality can surface some of our blind spots if we are honest. For example, we may learn that the criminal's mind and our own are not as far apart as we previously believed. G. K. Chesterton's fictional character Father Brown says he is able to solve crimes so well because his awareness of his own sin aids him in understanding the criminal mind.

In a terrific book on how to better read the Bible,[15] one of the authors describes the rebuke he received while teaching God's Word in Indonesia. It occurred during his first time of grading a multiple-choice exam for his students. He was perplexed by how many students left various questions unanswered. In the American context, students feel free to guess even when they don't have a clue as to the answer. Most Americans figure that they will most likely get lucky a few times and therefore get a better grade. The teacher, Randy Richards, was perplexed about the unanswered questions, so he proceeded to ask one of his students why they were leaving these multiple-choice questions unanswered. In fact, Richards told his student that he should have at least guessed. The student probably would have benefitted with a higher grade from doing so. What the student said caught Richards off guard: "What if I accidentally guessed the correct answer? I would be implying that I knew the answer when I didn't. That would be lying." We can learn much by traveling to distant places!

I made my own cultural gaffe during a teaching trip to Poland. I had dinner the night before the sessions began with a friend who invited me along with a dozen others. My friend is from the United States, but pretty much everyone else at dinner was born in Poland. I thought the polite thing to do was to ask lots of questions, so that's exactly what I did. I know that we Americans like to talk about ourselves, so I assumed the Poles were just like us. This was misguided American hubris—or at least of this American. After doing this for several minutes, my American friend leaned close to me and said, "I know you are trying to show love and respect, but Poles don't trust someone who never talks about himself." As an American, I was fine to shift and start talking about myself.

Detecting blind spots is also helped by the Christian understanding of sin. Carl Trueman underscores that Christian teaching on sin yields a greater sensitivity to power plays and manipulation while not allowing us to get lost in an endless sea of competing interpretations. It is this twin advantage that allows Christians to say "Yes, but . . ." to postmodern scholars like Michel Foucault.[16]

As Christians, we must be honest with what we discover from the historical record. It is always tempting to baptize our own ideas instead of looking more honestly at the complexity of the past. Justifying one's own loyalties when it comes to war shows how common the temptation is to overlook one's own misguided zeal, blind spots, and sin.[17] Travel and reading books that transport us to other times are helpful aids in detecting things we would not otherwise see.

Learning from Others: The Good, the Bad, and the Ugly

It is a wonderful blessing to read great books[18] by and about people who led compelling lives. One professor of English describes the regular experience of walking into his private study:

> I enter into the courts of these men, and they lovingly receive me. I ask them the reasons for their actions, and they courteously answer me. They remind me that shoddy standards of both piety and thought in our day are irrelevant to my work. They keep me from forgetting either whom I serve or *with* whom I serve. They are fellow lovers of Scripture and of the Lord, and they enrich my knowledge and experience of both.[19]

There is much to learn from others who went before us. However, it is a constant temptation to focus only on the good qualities of our favorite historical figures and look the other way when it comes to their weaknesses, poor judgment, and sin. Compelling models are wonderful to have, but we must remember they are human. In other words, we ought to heed Jesus's words that "no one is good—except God alone" (Luke 18:19).[20] It should be added that having a more accurate picture of our favorite saints reminds us that God uses "cracked pots." God uses all of us in spite of our imperfections—a great encouragement indeed.

Wise people learn from the mistakes of others. The unwise learn, if ever, only by personal experience. So by all means, learn from others, but remember the truth embodied in one title I like to use when teaching history: "Our rich, wonderful, and flawed past." It captures several important themes that must be kept in healthy tension. Too many Americans have an allergy to complexity. To be historically informed, one must be willing to face the multilayered realities of the past. Yes, there remains plenty that is black and white, but grays are in abundance as well.[21]

Growth in Discernment

I touched on this earlier, but here I will unpack it in more detail. A broad and deepening understanding of history builds discernment. History increases awareness of a myriad of dangers,[22] both subtle and not so subtle. Since we all need to navigate through these dangers, it is wise to grow in our understanding of human history. E. Michael Jones provides a good example:

> The communists, it turned out, were no more bound by the moral law than the Nazis, but they differed from the Nazis in the means that they employed to attain their ends. Unlike the Nazis, whose military conquest had been repelled, the communists achieved their ends while appearing to be our friends. Instead of overpowering us with force, the communists relied on subversion, on tunneling secretly through our institutions.[23]

Discernment also comes when we are able to distinguish between what is primary and what is secondary. Since worship pastors often get so much grief about their chosen style of music, I thought it appropriate to offer a test on the subject of worship here. Guess who said the "lifting up our hands in prayer is designed to remind us that we are far removed from God, unless our thoughts rise upward."[24] (No cheating by looking at the endnote.) You may be surprised to find out that this was none other than John Calvin. Our surprise is probably due to the impression of Calvin as a strongly cerebral type. But Calvin knew the history of the church, and this informed his life. Noted New Testament scholar Gordon Fee sheds additional light: "To lift up holy hands while in prayer is the assumed posture of prayer in both Judaism and early Christianity."[25] So when Paul said to "pray, lifting up holy hands" (1 Tim. 2:8 NASB), he was not talking about metaphorical hands. Therefore, both sides of the worship wars have something to learn. The pro hand-raisers need to realize the practice can be abused by emotionalism and wanting to be seen by men. In fact, one of our most important church fathers, Tertullian, warned about the potential abuses of raising one's hands in worship.[26] On the other side of this issue, those leery of raising their hands need to think more deeply about how physical posture can be an aid in worshipping God, and that it has a solid basis in the church's history.

Growing familiarity with great ideas, people, and movements greatly aids discernment. It helps us think through complex and controversial issues. As a pastor, I well remember a zealous couple who wanted to ban the book *I Know Why the Caged Bird Sings* by Maya Angelou. It was not required reading, but it was recommended for public high school students in our area. This couple came to my office one day to try and gain my support for their self-concocted campaign. They passionately described how the graphic details of Maya Angelou's book were offensive to them as Christians. I listened and then proceeded to ask some questions. Were they okay teaching their children about wars and all sorts of horrific events throughout history? If you start eliminating exposure to material simply based on its graphic nature, you will eliminate knowing a lot of history. And you will also eliminate knowing a lot of the Bible. The Bible talks about women boiling their babies to eat them, a woman who is sliced into twelve pieces, and much more.

Granted, there are things that fall under the *gratuitous* category and should not be read. For example, I know all I want to know about the Marquis de Sade, and I will never read his writings. However, I think Maya Angelou's book is something Christians can simply agree to disagree over. I have not read it and probably never will, but I would not necessarily fault another Christian for reading *I Know Why the Caged Bird Sings*.

My biggest concern with this couple's desire to ban the book revolved around their own inconsistency. They were not willing to ban the Bible, yet it has plenty of graphic accounts of human behavior at its worst. When I asked them how they would respond if someone raised this valid objection, they had no good answer.

One last example should drive home the benefit of how growth in historical understanding aids discernment. Listen to the words of historian George Marsden:

> I think ironically American evangelicals often seem to be more followers of Benjamin Franklin than they are of Jonathan Edwards. They [evangelicals] admire practicality, friendliness, moralisms, easy formulas, and quantifiable results. And while these Franklin-esque traits aren't all bad they sometimes contribute to evangelical superficiality. And we all know they are the equivalent of spiritual purveyors of junk food that have long capitalized on evangelicalism's market-driven economy.

Professor Marsden went on to say he had gone by a church sign during the Fourth of July that proclaimed, "The last four letters in American are I can."[27] In the same vein, Phil Vischer, the mastermind behind the wildly popular *VeggieTales* series, adds:

> The more I dove into Scripture, the more I realized I had been deluded. I had grown up drinking a dangerous cocktail—a mix of the gospel, the Protestant work ethic, and the American dream. . . . The Savior I was following seemed, in hindsight, equal parts Jesus, Ben Franklin, and Henry Ford.[28]

Reading history in tandem with the Bible *and* with others provides the best possible growth in discernment. And speaking of the importance of community . . .

Building Communities of Shared Memory

Tradition, that which is preserved and passed on from one person/group to another, is crucial for maintaining any culture.[29] We build "communities of memory"[30] by learning about our past. When there is no common memory,[31] there is no shared vocabulary, and the ability to understand one another is limited. The increasing historical amnesia of Europe with respect to their Christian heritage furnishes a sobering example. I saw this firsthand while teaching in France. It was difficult to find people who knew much about the French Huguenots or even John Calvin.[32]

I think a definition is in order. We throw around the word "community" but usually don't pause long enough to consider whether we properly understand what we are talking about. Too many believe that a homogeneous group of people is a community. It is not. It is what Robert Bellah and his associates aptly labeled a "lifestyle enclave."[33] "Lifestyle enclaves" are groups of people who desperately want to preserve a certain way of life by only being around those who share one another's socioeconomic status or race. This homogeneity stunts the ability to be challenged and changed for the better by those coming from a different background.

A community, especially a Christian one, is a group of people who share something in common that transcends socioeconomic or racial backgrounds. What Christians share is a common history—a living tradition. When we lose sight of this living tradition, we put ourselves in a perilous situation. With a sketchy understanding of our common identity as Christians, we are no longer able to have true community with one another.

One of my favorite books is *The Pilgrim's Progress* by John Bunyan. I don't know of any other book that captures so well what it means to grow as a Christian. Bunyan deftly describes Christians with various personalities and vulnerabilities. Even so, Bunyan urges that *all* true pilgrims avail themselves of certain practices. One of them is remembering what is worth remembering. *The Pilgrim's Progress* makes it clear that failing to remember what is most important can get you into all sorts of trouble. Bunyan also underscores the importance of being in community with wise people. Not only should pilgrims desire friends as companions en route to the Celestial City, pilgrims are also wise to have people along the way who can offer sage counsel. One must be developing one's discernment here, as Bunyan makes clear that there are many people along the way who are foolish and bent on getting true pilgrims off the right path.

Some Christians are confused over how to understand and certainly apply the idea of tradition. The origins of the word describe that which has been "handed over" throughout history.

Karl Marx understood the power of tradition:

> Men make their own history; but they do not make it just as they please; they do not make it under circumstances chosen by themselves, but under circumstances directly found, given and transmitted from the past. The tradition of all the dead generations weighs like a nightmare on the brain of the living.[34]

Carl Trueman reflects on Marx's insight: "Marx's point is that everyone lives at a particular time in a particular place; and that context imposes limits upon them: geographical, economic, conceptual, linguistic, etc." Trueman adds that pretending any of us "somehow stand outside of history . . . is thus hopelessly naïve."[35]

David McCullough says we are "ungrateful" if we fail to remember those who have blazed the path before us.[36] When we get to know these individuals, it allows us to have a bond, irrespective of differences like ethnicity or socioeconomic standing. This kind of unity allows for greater confidence and stability as we make our way through life.

Church potlucks and small group fellowship are wonderful ways to enjoy Christian community, but they must be anchored in a common tradition. Otherwise, our church will not be much different than the local Elks Club.

History Offers Hope

Hope, of course, must be grounded in truth. Twisting events by papering over the darker realities of the past is unwise and does not lead to a mature understanding of human history. Professor Wilfred McClay adds these important words: "The dark side is always an important part of the truth, just as everything that is solid casts a shadow when placed in the light." McClay also says that those who believe in original sin probably have a leg up on getting an accurate account of what transpired.[37] As Christians, we can honestly scour the historical record and not be timid about what may be found, even (and especially so) with respect to our "heroes." Christian teaching allows us to have a realistic view of human nature, along with confidence that all people are capable of noble deeds. We should never be surprised by the dark and sinister things people do, nor the acts of heroism and generosity.

History Does Not Repeat Itself, but It Does Rhyme

Mark Twain penned the oft-quoted words of this heading. It reminds us that historical events are not identical, yet they reflect human nature, which remains constant. The packaging of human events is different, but the struggles and triumphs are all too familiar. One military historian uses an ancient example to remind us of this connection:

> Human nature being what it is, we citizens of the West often want to enjoy our bounty and retreat into private lives—to go home, eat pizza, and watch television. This is nothing new. I would refer you to Petronius's *Satyricon*, a banquet scene written around 60 A.D. about affluent Romans who make fun of the soldiers who are up on the Rhine protecting them. This is what Rome had become. And it's not easy

> to convince someone who has the good life to fight against someone who doesn't.[38]

This indeed sounds very up to date. Simply recall what George Bush said shortly after the devastating events of 9/11. He understandably wanted Americans to not be immobilized by fear, but unfortunately conveyed the wrong message. He told us to "get down to Disney World in Florida. Take your families and enjoy life—the way we want it to be enjoyed."

Kept from "Chronological Snobbery"

"Chronological snobbery"[39] is the way C. S. Lewis characterized his once-held arrogance when he, in the words of Allan Bloom, believed that "the here and now is all there is."[40] Other ways of describing this antihistorical impulse include seeing modern men as "momentary men,"[41] "the complacent world of the perpetual present,"[42] and "nowism."[43] Those who choose not to grow in their knowledge of history will find themselves "stranded in the present."[44] I prefer to say *stuck* in the present, as it seems a bit more hopeful than stranded. There is indeed a way out. To bring in Bunyan again, his main character, Christian, got stuck (not stranded) in the Slough of Despond.

History is, as David McCullough puts it, "an antidote to the hubris of the present—the idea that everything we have and everything we do and everything we think is the ultimate, the best."[45] All of us modern folk tend to think that our era has "progressed" more than all the previous eras. This raises a serious issue. We gladly assume our modern notions of progress like speed, efficiency, and technology are superior, yet we rarely stop to explain why they are better than the dynamics of other eras. I am grateful for central air conditioning, indoor plumbing, and the rest, but I am arrogant if I think there are no real dangers in various aspects of modern life. It is only by familiarizing myself (while maintaining a teachable spirit) with other eras of human history that I can see the things my own modern culture may not be doing so well. A destructive disregard for wanting to grow in one's literacy of the past is the path of the foolish.

Driving to the Future Requires Looking in the Rearview Mirror

It is dangerous to drive down a road without regularly looking in the rearview mirror, and it is the same with moving ahead in our lives. Postman puts it well:

> I am suspicious of people who want us to be forward-looking. I literally do not know what they mean when they say, "We must look ahead to see where we are going." What is it that they wish us to look at? There is nothing yet to see in the future. If looking ahead means anything, it must mean finding in our past useful and humane ideas with which to fill the future.[46]

Renowned atheist Camille Paglia echoes the same sentiment: "It is the past, not the dizzy present, that is the best door to the future."[47] Our reluctance to look back may actually mask the real problem—our desire for autonomy. It can be threatening to look back at real people and real events. Those realities cannot be changed. Many of them challenge us to live more nobly, which is not the sort of thing most of us want to consider doing. The future allows us to dream up whatever reality we would like. G. K. Chesterton said the past gave us real models of noble living. The future doesn't threaten us because there is no one there who can force us to reevaluate our own lives. By definition, they do not yet exist. Chesterton adds, "In front of us lies an unknown or unreal world which we can mold according to every cowardice or triviality in our temperaments."[48] In the same spirit as Chesterton, philosopher John Kaag speaks of being struck by the idea that history is "irrevocable . . . unchangeable, adamantine, the safest of storehouses, the home of the eternal ages."[49] Kaag reminds us that adamantine was "an unbreakable metal from the mythical past."[50]

History is not a wax nose. We must honestly assess the villains and the heroes, not to mention that many had characteristics of both. We also face the most daunting prospect of all: looking honestly at our own lives in light of previous luminaries, determining how we compare and where we can grow and do better.

Discussion Questions

1. Discuss the following insight from Professor Mark Noll: "It is the Word of God who became flesh that encourages Bible-believing evangelicals to look seriously at the realm of the flesh, for to learn about that realm is to learn about the sphere of God's fullest manifestation of himself."

2. Which historical figures do you admire the most? Can you name some of their weaknesses?

3. Do you enjoy a true Christian community, or is it more of a "lifestyle enclave?"

4. Is it correct to assume, among other things, that studying history is threatening because it provides us with real models of courage and conviction who challenge us to take an honest inventory of our own lives?

Notes

[1]See Richard Lederer, "56 B.C. and All That," *National Review*, March 1, 1993, 51–52. I left the misspellings intact.

[2]Jim Collins, "Book Value," January 1996. Also see "The Classics" (December 1996) and "The Learning Executive" (August 1997). All are available at www.jimcollins.com.

[3]The book Peters chose was *Adams vs. Jefferson: The Tumultuous Election of 1800*, by John Ferling, posted at www.tompeters.com (July 25, 2006).

[4]Steven B. Sample, *The Contrarian's Guide to Leadership* (San Francisco: Jossey-Bass, 2002), 55–70. The title of one chapter captures Sample's conviction: "You Are What You Read." The *New York Times* carried a fascinating piece on the reading habits of certain high-level executives. Among other things, the article underscored how great books impact these executives personally and how they look to hire those who also love quality

reading material. One company owner favored hiring managers who love poetry! See Harriet Rubin, "C.E.O. Libraries Reveal Keys to Success," *New York Times*, July 21, 2007.

[5]See Stephen R. Covey, *The 7 Habits of Highly Effective People* (New York: Simon & Schuster, 1989), 296. I benefited from reading this book and the follow-up volume of sorts, *First Things First*. I do have serious concerns about Covey's persistent assumption that knowledge alone can bring transformation. See David George Moore, *Confident Living: How to Discover God's Will for Your Life* (Austin: Two Cities Ministries, 2000), 2–3; David George Moore, "Challenging the Pursuit of Greatness: Jim Collins' *Good to Great*," *Patheos*, September 27, 2010, and David George Moore, *Pooping Elephants, Mowing Weeds: What Business Gurus Failed to Tell You* (self-pub., Amazon Digital Services, 2018), Kindle.

[6]That interview can be seen in its entirety at www.mooreengaging.com.

[7]Tony Horwitz, "Clio's Craft: History and Storytelling" (presentation in session 38 of the 127th annual meeting of the American Historical Association, New Orleans, January 3–6, 2013).

[8]C. S. Lewis, *Surprised by Joy* (New York: Harcourt Brace & Co., 1984), 236.

[9]Ronald H. Nash, *Christian Faith and Historical Understanding* (Grand Rapids: Zondervan, 1984), 11–12, and John Warwick Montgomery, *Where Is History Going?* (Minneapolis: Bethany Fellowship, 1969), 7–8.

[10]Mark A. Noll, *The Scandal of the Evangelical Mind* (Grand Rapids: William B. Eerdmans, 1994), 55. Many Christians are still in need of persuasion on this issue.

[11]Michael Horton, "The New Gnosticism: Is It the Age of the Spirit or the Spirit of the Age?," *Modern Reformation* 4, no. 4 (July/Aug. 1995): 4–12; emphasis mine.

[12]A. W. Tozer, *Whatever Happened to Worship?* (Camp Hill, PA: Christian Publications, 1985), 49–50.

[13]For a classic work that wisely describes "blind spots," see Reinhold Niebuhr, *The Irony of American History* (Chicago: University of Chicago Press, 2008).

[14]Forrest McDonald, "The Speech: Address to Last Class Taught as a Regular Member of the Faculty at the University of Alabama," UA Department of History, n.d., www.as.ua.edu/history/mcdonald.html; emphasis in original.

[15]E. Randolph Richards and Brandon J. O'Brien, *Misreading Scripture with Western Eyes* (Downers Grove, IL: InterVarsity Press, 2012), 20.

[16]Carl R. Trueman, "Reckoning with the Past in an Anti-historical Age," *Themelios* 23 (February 1998): 2.

[17]Four books have helped me here, covering three of the United States' major wars. One is on the Revolutionary War, two cover the Civil War, and one looks at World War I. See James P. Byrd, *Sacred Scripture, Sacred War:*

The Bible and the American Revolution (New York: Oxford University Press, 2013); Mark A. Noll, *The Civil War as a Theological Crisis* (Chapel Hill: University of North Carolina Press, 2006); George C. Rable, *God's Almost Chosen Peoples: A Religious History of the American Civil War* (Chapel Hill: University of North Carolina Press, 2010); and Philip Jenkins, *The Great and Holy War: How World War I Became a Religious Crusade* (New York: HarperCollins, 2014). My interviews with all these authors, except Noll, can be found on *Patheos/Jesus Creed.*

[18] I highly recommend "On the Reading of Old Books" by C. S. Lewis. It can be found in C. S. Lewis, *God in the Dock* (Grand Rapids: William B. Eerdmans, 1970), and in the introduction to St. Athanasius, *On the Incarnation* (Crestwood, NY: St. Vladimir's Orthodox Theological Seminary, 1993). Also see the comments of T. S. Eliot in Douglas Wilson, *Recovering the Lost Tools of Learning* (Wheaton, IL: Crossway Books, 1991), 85.

[19] Donald T. Williams, "The Great Conversation," *Alliance Life*, March 17, 1993, 7. I am grateful to Dr. Bern Jackson, who frequently supplied me with this magazine.

[20] *Hagiography* is the technical term historians use for writing that just emphasizes the positive aspects of people and fails to mention the negative—or at least significantly downplays the negative's importance. Hagiography is the combination of two Greek words that refer to writing about saints or holy ones. For a good discussion of this temptation among Christians, see Carl R. Trueman, "Ferret Breeding on Watership Down," *Reformation21*, June 30, 2006, 4–5. Trueman offers wise counsel on having a "humble and critical engagement with history" (p. 5) and the ever-present problem of being selective by choosing to focus on the perceived merits of certain things we like. For example, it is common for many of us to assume that free market capitalism is always a pure and unadulterated good (see pp. 3–4).

[21] For a good example, see Allen C. Guelzo, *Redeeming the Great Emancipator* (Cambridge, MA: Harvard University Press, 2016), 91.

[22] Inhumane practices are the logical outcome when the importance of history is jettisoned. See George Weigel, *The Cube and the Cathedral* (New York: Basic Books, 2005), 20–21.

[23] E. Michael Jones, *Monsters from the Id* (Dallas: Spence, 2000), 190.

[24] John Calvin, *Institutes of the Christian Religion*, trans. Henry Beveridge (Grand Rapids: William B. Eerdmans, 1983), III.XX.V.

[25] Gordon D. Fee, *1 and 2 Timothy, Titus: New International Biblical Commentary* (Peabody, MA: Hendrickson, 1988), 71; also see 76.

[26] See Tertullian's *On Prayer*, section 17. I am grateful to Gordon Fee for pointing me to Tertullian's work. Tertullian's warnings demonstrate how

pervasive the practice was in the early church of raising one's hands to God in worship.

[27]George Marsden, "The Legacy of Jonathan Edwards" (lecture, Beeson Divinity School, Birmingham, AL, November 12, 2004). I am grateful to Professor Thomas Kidd for drawing my attention to this lecture.

[28]As quoted in Skye Jethani, *With: Reimaging the Way You Relate to God* (Nashville: Thomas Nelson, 2011), 90.

[29]Allan Bloom, *The Closing of the American Mind* (New York: Simon & Schuster, 1987), 27.

[30]Robert N. Bellah, Richard Madsen, William M. Sullivan, Ann Swidler, and Steven M. Tipton, *Habits of the Heart* (New York: Harper & Row, 1985), 153.

[31]See the insight of Robert M. Hutchins in Jim Nelson Black, *When Nations Die* (Wheaton, IL: Tyndale House, 1994), 147.

[32]For more, see the eloquent requiem (with the possibility of resurrection) by Weigel, *The Cube and the Cathedral.* From the Romantic movement to the present, the breaking away from tradition has been in vogue among the academic guild. See Donald Kagan, "In Defense of History" (34th Jefferson Lecture in the Humanities, Washington, DC, May 12, 2005), pp. 2–3, www.neh.gov/whoweare/kagan/lecture.html.

[33]Bellah et al., *Habits of the Heart*, 71–75.

[34]As quoted in Trueman, "Ferret Breeding on Watership Down," 2.

[35]Trueman, "Ferret Breeding on Watership Down," 2–3.

[36]David McCullough, "Knowing History and Knowing Who We Are," *Imprimis* 34 (April 2005): 2.

[37]Wilfred M. McClay, *A Student's Guide to U.S. History* (Wilmington, DE: ISI Books, 2002), 10.

[38]Victor Davis Hanson, "The Future of Western War," *Imprimis* 38 (November 2009): 5.

[39]See Lewis, *Surprised by Joy*, 206–8.

[40]Bloom, *Closing of the American Mind*, 64.

[41]Andrew Lytle's designation. As quoted in Douglas Jones and Douglas Wilson, *Angels in the Architecture* (Moscow, ID: Canon Press, 1998), 98.

[42]Trueman, "Ferret Breeding on Watership Down," 6.

[43]Paul Persall's term. As quoted in Richard Winter, *Still Bored in a Culture of Entertainment* (Wheaton, IL: Crossway Books, 2002), 116.

[44]From the title of a book by Peter Fritzsche. As quoted in Margaret Bendroth, *The Spiritual Practice of Remembering* (Grand Rapids: William B. Eerdmans, 2013), 13.

[45]McCullough, "Knowing History," 5.

[46]Neil Postman, *Building a Bridge to the Eighteenth Century* (New York: Alfred A. Knopf, 1999), 13.

[47] As quoted in Brad Miner, *The Compleat Gentleman* (Dallas: Spence, 2004), 207, cf. 100.

[48] As quoted in Ralph C. Wood, "Creating a Christian Educational Culture amidst a Multicultural and Anticultural Age," Lilly Colloquium on Christian Education (March 24, 2001), 7–8, http://homepages.baylor.edu/ralph_wood. Professor Wood's site contains a treasure trove of wonderful essays. He indicates that the quote sounds like Chesterton, but he has not been able to locate it. See Ralph C. Wood, *Contending for the Faith: The Church's Engagement with Culture* (Waco, TX: Baylor University Press, 2003), 207.

[49] Josiah Royce is being quoted by Kaag here. See John Kaag, *American Philosophy: A Love Story* (New York: Farrar, Straus and Giroux, 2016), 190.

[50] Kaag, *American Philosophy*, 190.

CHAPTER THREE

WHAT CAN WE REALLY KNOW ABOUT THE PAST?

All history becomes subjective; in other words there is properly no history, only biography. **—Ralph Waldo Emerson**

In the study of history, I have come to believe, it is always dangerous to assume that men do not mean what they say, that words are a façade which must be penetrated in order to arrive at some fundamental but hidden reality. **—Edmund S. Morgan**

The current fad of skepticism and relativism is as old as the Sophists of ancient Greece and had a great revival with the Pyrrhonism of the sixteenth century. On both occasions their paradoxical and self-contradictory glamour yielded in time to common sense and the massive evidence that some searches are more objective, some things are truer than others, however elusive perfect objectivity and truth may be. **—Donald Kagan**

Historiography is a word you may not have run across before. You can see that it has something to do with "writing about history." Without getting too technical, one's commitment to a specific historiography[1] reveals how past events will be interpreted. For example, some may see God intimately involved in the drafting of the US Constitution. Others believe the Constitution is a woefully inadequate document, an artifact of flawed men. And still others may tie that inadequacy to the fact that only men were involved directly in drafting it. So how does one determine who is correct? One side may be closer to the truth than the others, perhaps none are in the ballpark of reality, or all three positions may have landed on some important insights worth pondering. How then does one go about reconstructing the past in a responsible way? Though it seems like a rather daunting task, this chapter is dedicated to addressing it.

There is an irony of sorts to the study of history. Many of us tend to think the past is much more difficult to understand than the present. There is a sense, of course, where this is true. Professor Gary Gallagher likes to remind his students that history is much more complex than they probably originally thought. He counsels that "anyone who wants simple answers should not take a history class."

We should also appreciate that deciphering our own time carries its own particular set of challenges. As mentioned earlier, we tend to assume that all features of the twenty-first century, like its technological advances, are always a net positive. It is difficult to be detached observers with our own time when the wow factor of things like technological gizmos and gadgets surrounds us. This leads some to conclude that it is easier, in many ways, to understand the past. It is during the present, or what David Wells calls "our time,"[2] where the "trivial and profound" seem to "strike you with the same intensity."[3] Sorting out the trivial from the profound can be challenging. The news regularly juxtaposes the trivial (an update on some pop icon) with the profound (the Syrian refugee crisis). Few seem ashamed anymore at the absurdity. Ascertaining what really matters, both in the present as well as the past, certainly has its challenges.

Selectivity Does Not Mean *Subjectivity*

As mentioned in Chapter One, reconstructing history is always selective in nature.[4] Insignificant events like Henry VIII sneezing should not be included.[5] *Selectivity* does not mean understanding the past becomes a purely subjective expression of the historian's fancy. Everyone appreciates that when a court of law requires a witness to give "the truth, the whole truth, and nothing but the truth," *relevant, not exhaustive,* information (which is impossible) is in view. If the data are collected carefully by reading the relevant primary sources, a variety of scholars are consulted to make sure one's bias doesn't color the evidence, and there is a willingness to submit one's work to others for review, then there can be "proper confidence" (to use Lesslie Newbigin's description) that one has landed on a reliable account of events.[6]

To ensure that an author has written wisely, I regularly consult book reviews by leading scholars. When a variety of scholars use words like "careful," "balanced," "judicious," and "the author is familiar with the primary and secondary sources" to describe a historian's writing, you can be confident that it is a responsible work. This is especially the case when a reviewer disagrees with the conclusions of the author but still finds the scholarship sound.

Shoddy scholarship and personal bias will eventually be snuffed out.[7] A good example is Michael Bellesiles's book *Arming America: The Origins of a National Gun Culture,* published in 2000. It won the prestigious Bancroft Prize, awarded by Columbia University for the best books in history, biography, and diplomacy. But Bellesiles's work started to raise questions. His use of data to prove that there were fewer guns in the antebellum period than is commonly thought initially sparked the controversy. Eventually he was found "guilty of unprofessional and misleading work." He had to resign his professorship at Emory in October 2002. Columbia University also rescinded the Bancroft Prize—the first time it did so in its history.

On the other side of the ledger, consider a book about Jonathan Edwards, *A God Entranced Vision of All Things*.[8] It shows balanced scholarship done with integrity. Though the editors believe Edwards was both a "profound and sound" theologian, they invited Sherard Burns to contribute a chapter titled "Trusting the Theology of a Slave Owner." That chapter, as one of the editors described in the introduction, avoided "easy exoneration"[9] of Edwards's behavior. Burns doesn't dismiss the contributions of Edwards. In fact, Burns, who is African American and committed to the reformed expression of Christianity, calls Edwards one of his "heroes." He talks about how slavery was "socially ingrained" during the time of Edwards. That is certainly a historical fact, but Burns does not mention it to get Edwards off the hook. He does so to alert us to the historical conditions but underscores that others living at the same time found everything about slavery repugnant. That was true among various Americans, and it was also true of various people living in other parts of the world, like England. For the latter, one thinks of John Wesley's vigorous opposition to slavery. And ironically, Wesley was born in the same year as Edwards. One cannot easily explain away Edwards's embrace of slavery, though readers walk away from Burns's chapter with an appreciation for the tremendous contributions of Jonathan Edwards but are reminded, once again, that all of us have "feet of clay."

Yes, all recounting of the past is selective.[10] We must remember that even the gospel writers were selective in their accounts.[11] As John described many years ago, there were "many other things" Jesus did that were not recorded (John 21:25). However, these realities do not imply that we should bypass or smooth over the parts of history that make us feel embarrassed or uncomfortable.

Faith versus Reason: A Sacred Untruth

It is common for people to drive a wedge between faith and reason. Framing matters in this way leads us to accept that some live mainly by faith while others rely on reason. Religious folks supposedly take it on faith alone that the world was created by God.[12] Non-religious types supposedly hold to reason, which leads them to conclude that the world is a result of purely materialistic forces. For them, "The cosmos is," as Carl Sagan famously put it, "all that is or ever was or ever will be."

Biblically, the true dichotomy is not between faith and reason, but faith and sight.[13] The Bible is full of appeals to right thinking. For example, even a cursory read through the book of Acts reveals how much the apostle Paul utilized reason in his own ministry.

Overstating the difference between faith and reason (or faith and knowledge) has been with us for many years.[14] Christian philosopher Ronald Nash offers this corrective: "Genuine faith does not exist in a cognitive vacuum. In everyday life, we proportion faith and trust to the evidences. . . . *Believing against reason is credulity, not faith*."[15]

Everyday life lends itself to more of a dynamic interplay between faith and reason. In other words, we place our faith in certain clues or evidence that our mind deems to be reasonable. One scholar helpfully distills the work of Samuel Butler on this issue:

> Butler reminded us that a total devotion to duty—shown, for example, by leaping into a river to save a drowning child—could *and reasonably*, be associated with many empirical uncertainties and probabilities: we might be mistaken about the strength of the current, about our swimming ability, or whether in fact that floating heap was a child, and so on. But acknowledging these uncertainties Butler claimed that we should nevertheless think a man in a literal sense distracted . . . who failed to respond to the moral challenge displayed by such a situation of great consequence.[16]

Esther Meek provides a good description of the dynamic interplay between faith and reason: "Knowing is the responsible human struggle to rely on clues to focus on a coherent pattern and submit to its reality."[17] Meek uses the example of how she found a reliable mechanic based on important clues she had gathered. My own experience in finding a mechanic I trust was based on the gushing reviews of two close friends. Both gave rave reviews about how Joe Ruiz saved them money and did a great job on their respective cars. My confidence to trust in Joe's character and competence was greatly aided by the testimonies of my two friends.

No one is immune from using both faith and reason. Marxist scholar Terry Eagleton makes this abundantly clear in his critique of infamous atheist Richard Dawkins:

> Dawkins considers that all faith is blind faith, and that Christian and Muslim children are brought up to believe unquestioningly. Not even the dim-witted clerics who knocked me about at grammar school thought that. For mainstream Christianity, reason, argument and honest doubt have always played an integral role in belief. . . . Reason, to be sure, doesn't go all the way down for believers, but it doesn't for most sensitive, civilized non-religious types either. Even Richard Dawkins lives more by faith than by reason. We hold many beliefs that have no unimpeachably rational justification, but are nonetheless reasonable to entertain.[18]

Properly understanding the past is hardly the subjective endeavor Emerson described in the quote that starts off this chapter. We can find many reliable witnesses that help us reconstruct what happened. It makes sense why Emerson chalked everything up to subjective whim. He did not want to be tethered to any tradition.[19] Emerson gladly elevated the autonomous individual. He, and others who followed in his wake, wanted to create their own tradition. The notion of submitting oneself to something bigger than the individual was a noxious idea. Perhaps this kind of posture today tells us why so many do not want to study history.

If we are paying attention, we can see that the interplay between faith and reason is constantly with us. Why do we step into an elevator? Perhaps the cable will break—this has happened for a few unfortunate folks. Perhaps the elevator will get stuck—this has happened more often than the cable breaking, but it is still rare. We step into elevators because we pick up on clues that it is reliable to trust their proper functioning. Most of us who step inside are not experts on the inner workings of elevators. We trust that competent people are behind their proper functioning. But how do we know this for certain? We don't, yet we still step inside, unless some overwhelming fear comes upon us. We also may observe that other seemingly sane people are confident that the elevator works properly. But again, how do we know these folks are sane? Maybe the people stepping into the elevator have a death wish and have conspired together to commit group suicide. We go with our clues based on reason and trust that these folks seem to want to live. They seem to be excited about the day. We pick up other clues, like hearing a cheerful conversation between a couple about an upcoming vacation. And on it goes. Most of the time, our utilization of faith and reason occurs very quickly. This twin relationship of faith and reason is impossible to resist in daily life.

In clarifying the dynamic interplay between faith and reason,[20] we must remember that historical knowledge is still different from scientific proof—a point to which we now turn to better understand.

History and Science Are Different Disciplines

It is obviously impossible to go into a lab and repeat the events of Napoleon at Waterloo or Lincoln writing the Gettysburg Address. The ability to repeat one's experiment is characteristic of certain types of scientific investigations, but not of history. However, this should not lead us to conclude that only science is rational or "objective" in nature.[21] Wilfred McClay comments on how historians ought to proceed in ways that mimic the work of responsible scientists. McClay commends "the fastidious gathering and sifting of evidence, the effort to be dispassionate and evenhanded, the openness to alternative hypothesis and explanations, the caution in propounding sweeping generalizations."

Though we "draw upon history's traditional storytelling structure, we also can use sophisticated analytical models to discover patterns and regularities in individual and collective behavior." But history as a discipline does have important distinctions from science. These may be intuitive to us, but they are not always well articulated. McClay offers vivid imagery to help us recall the differences between history and science. History "cannot devise replicable experiments, and still claim to be studying human beings, rather than corpses."[22] On the other side of things, scientists need to acknowledge that they themselves are not robots, though some of us may be tempted to think otherwise. They are human beings, so the goal of 100 percent objectivity is not achievable.

Steve Sample is not only well-known for his stellar work as president of the University of Southern California; he is also an inventor. He understands the elusive nature of total objectivity:

> To be fair, no human being, not even the most disciplined scientist, can begin an investigation without having his mind at least partially made up from the outset. Francis Bacon in the sixteenth century believed that scientists (called natural philosophers in those days) should simply collect observations and facts in a totally neutral way, and that eventually patterns and scientific laws would "leap from the page,"

> so to speak. As it happens, though, Bacon was wrong. Every scientist, and every investigative reporter, starts out with a hypothesis in mind and then tries to collect facts and observations in support of that hypothesis. Neither the scientist nor the reporter is being objective at this point.[23]

We must keep in mind that our scientist friends *who believe* (the word is instructive) only materialistic causes[24] are responsible for all that exists do so out of a certain hypothesis. For example, scientists can't disprove miracles, but they regularly *assume* they are silly to believe in if you are going to be enlightened.[25] Evidence for how the world came into existence must be interpreted, and that is not a purely objective matter. Furthermore, the beginning of the universe is not repeatable, so even the most ardent atheist must concede that everyone makes certain assumptions about the origins of the world we now inhabit. Some, like a doctoral student in microbiology I met years ago at Stanford University, may attempt to dodge the issue. This budding scholar insisted that he was only interested in "science," not the *philosophy* of science. He believed that musing about the origins of the world was a waste of time and kept him from doing science as he conceived it. Unfortunately, his decision to not pay philosophy any mind only resulted in a less thoughtful philosophy of science. John Maynard Keynes observed that trying to free ourselves from the perceived shackles of philosophy only results in becoming "slaves of some defunct philosopher."[26] It reminds me of when people say they are not interested in philosophy because they are so "practically minded," yet fail to realize that pragmatism is a philosophy. Indeed, all humans use both faith *and* reason in arriving at their dearly held views—or, more accurately, beliefs.

It may seem strange to us now, but there was a time in the not-too-distant past when an eminent Puritan like Cotton Mather could be elected to a prestigious academy of sciences like the Royal Society of London.[27] Granted, Mather was elected for his cutting-edge work on inoculations, but his belief in the Christian God was no barrier to being treated with wide acclaim.

To be sure, historians and scientists approach their work differently, but the best of both have a desire to look at the data with the utmost amount of care while ever aware that they can't totally divorce themselves from every personal bias.

Judeo-Christian Contributions to Understanding History

We may not be fully aware of how significant the contributions of the Judeo-Christian worldview are to the understanding of history. Let me briefly sketch a few of them here. First is the linear view of time. Robert Royal puts this very well, so I offer a fuller quote here:

> In fact, we have to say candidly that it was the most recent discoveries of modern science itself that confirmed the religious intuitions about linear time that first arose with Abraham and his journey from Ur of the Chaldees. In many ways, the slow emergence of the consequences of such truths was to be expected. Christians and Jews still lived a life that largely followed the pattern of the seasons, even if both of them expected God to lead them through history towards a fulfillment in the end times. . . . It is much easier to

> accept novelty and change, indeed to pursue them consciously, if you also believe that the Creator goes with you on every path, as readers of the Bible in all ages believed. Indeed, such unprecedented developments are called for by the biblical idea of sacred history. God himself says so openly: "I will lead the blind by a path they do not know, by paths they have not known I will guide them. . . . I will not forsake them." (Isa. 42:16)[28]

Biblical scholar Scott Hahn adds:

> The modern Western approach to history is antithetical to the ancient Near Eastern perspective. If the modern view is linear, progressive, optimistic, and secular, the ancient outlook tended to be cyclical, regressive, pessimistic, and mythical. Meanwhile, the biblical outlook falls somewhere between both extremes.[29]

In addition to the reality of linear time, Christians are well prepared to "expect the unexpected." The quote by Royal above makes this clear. Consider miracles. By definition, they are unexpected events. Materialists who expect a steady progression of events are not well prepared for the unexpected. It is also true that unexpected events, when they include evil and suffering, can throw even the most devout, but Christians have candid teaching on the subject throughout their most important document, the Bible.[30] Where can materialists go for answers that don't paper over the struggle yet still offer hope?

Hope is another advantage Christians have in understanding history. Unfortunately, hope is regularly bandied about by us Christians in sloppy ways. It is easy to assume we know the biblical boundaries of certain words, especially those that get used the most frequently. I am thinking here of words like faith, hope, and love. I have found many Christians unclear on what biblical hope entails. If we are not clear on the proper meaning of hope, it would be wise to spend some time digging into the Scriptures. Clarifying what the Christian faith means by hope is time well spent. Christian hope is not a flimsy expectation or an uncertain wish for how we desire the future to turn out. Christian hope is grounded in the promises of God—promises that we can count on (2 Cor. 1:20). Hope is not grounded in guessing. Hope is grounded in the good promises of a trustworthy God. This kind of hope is different than the one regularly invoked by people who don't have a biblical hope. A hope that is grounded in God's promises understands that human history is moving inexorably toward the revelation of God's kingdom in all its glory. Human history is full of nasty stuff that causes us to lose heart, but Christians can be confident that God's good purposes will all be fulfilled. That is a hope worth living and dying for!

As Now, So Then?

One temptation too many fall prey to is "presentism." This occurs when a current or modern understanding is foisted on an idea or person of the past.[31] Here I will provide some examples from eminent scholars. This alerts us as to how vulnerable anyone can be to making this mistake. For example, Arthur Schlesinger Jr. was probably guilty of conceiving of American history as "the steady progress of pragmatic liberalism."[32] The great Perry Miller cast the eighteenth-century theologian Jonathan Edwards as a twentieth-century thinker.[33]

Some examples are absurd. These sorts of claims are not made by respected scholars. Trying to make the case that Abraham Lincoln was a homosexual is a good example. If one studies the social history of the nineteenth century, it becomes clear that this notion is simply the result of personal agendas, overactive imaginations, and assuming our current taboos were operative during Lincoln's time. Joshua Shenk adds, "Because Lincoln and [Joshua] Speed were so intimate, and shared a bed, people sometimes assume they were homosexual." If this were the criteria, Shenk adds that "precious few men in the early nineteenth century would *not* be called gay."[34]

We must guard against the assumption that our modern notions are seamless with those of the past and allow the past to speak to us from its own vantage point. Many like to remind us that the strangeness of the past must be able to speak in a way that is consistent with what truly took place.

History as a Quest for Truth

Karl Popper was an Austrian-born Jew. He believed it was dangerous to see history as having any ultimate meaning. It is understandable why he came to such a conclusion. Popper "fled from the Nazi occupation of Vienna. The Nazis, like the Marxists, justified their actions in terms of the purpose they saw in history."[35] Concocting the purpose that suits one's selfish, even cruel, aspirations is not unique to the Nazis. Nazis were infamous for doing this, but they are hardly alone in the annals of history.

Popper's fear has been realized on too many occasions, but the study of history, properly understood, can and should be a search for the truth. One discovery made by American political theorist William Dunning highlights this well. Dunning discovered that "Andrew Johnson's first message to Congress was actually drafted by George Bancroft." Dunning wrote to his wife that it may be difficult for her to "form any idea of the pleasure it gives me to have discovered this little historical fact." Gertrude Himmelfarb adds further commentary: "Every serious historian has had this experience—the pleasure of discovering a fact that may appear in the published work in a subordinate clause or footnote, but that, however trivial in itself, validates the entire enterprise, *because it is not only new but also true*."[36]

One of my own experiences was finding an error in a major reference work on American history. In *The Oxford Guide to the United States*, edited by Paul S. Boyer, there is an error in the entry on John Winthrop. It says Winthrop had three wives and lost two. Actually, Winthrop had four wives and was a widower three times. Boyer did not write the entry, but he quickly thanked me via email and said future editions would be corrected. Boyer's quick response demonstrates a desire to write responsible history. My own experiences of reading and interacting with many historians give me confidence that most are seeking to discover the truth. In other words, most do not play fast and loose with the truth, as we saw earlier with the former professor Michael Bellesiles.

In her terrific book on ancient Rome, Mary Beard offers fascinating examples of new discoveries in archaeology.[37] These paint a fuller picture of various aspects of ancient Roman culture and its people. Beard is quick to say that contemporary historians having access to these new discoveries does not mean that prior historians were not good historians.

No historian will ever know all that can describe a particular time and place. New histories, in the sense that we have either new discoveries or make new connections with what we already know, are being made every day. In that sense, all history is an ever-unfolding revelation (and revision rightly understood) of what occurred. And yet we can be confident that there are ample documents and records to provide an accurate picture of the past.

Discussion Questions

1. What are some instances in the book of Acts where Paul utilizes reason in his approach to ministry?

2. What takes more faith: being an atheist or being a Christian?

3. In what way(s) did the description of science by Steven Sample help you clarify the proper boundaries of that discipline?

4. What examples of "presentism" have you seen? Have you ever been guilty of it?

Notes

[1]A helpful overview is Paul S. Boyer, ed., *The Oxford Guide to United States History* (New York: Oxford University Press, 2001), s.v. "Historiography, American," by John Higham. Also, see Nancy F. Partner, "Historiography," http://cuhist.wordpress.com/historiography.

[2]See his seminal work: David Wells, *No Place for Truth, or Whatever Happened to Evangelical Theology?* (Grand Rapids: William B. Eerdmans, 1993).

[3]Interview with David F. Wells, May 15, 2005, www.9marks.com.

[4]Carl R. Trueman, *Histories and Fallacies* (Wheaton, IL: Crossway Books, 2010), 21 and 69–70.

[5]See Ronald H. Nash, *Christian Faith and Historical Understanding* (Grand Rapids: Zondervan, 1984), 13.

[6]I have posted hundreds of reviews on Amazon. It is a wonderful platform, but reviews there should be read with discernment. There are many helpful reviews posted there, but the personal agendas of some can also be found. Among the egregious examples are "reviews" about the poor delivery of a book or how the Kindle edition is poorly formatted. These are not book reviews. The most absurd "review" I've seen to date was a "reviewer" who said quite candidly that he had not read the book but still did not like it!

[7]For examples, see Elizabeth Fox-Genovese, "Advocacy and the Writing of American Women's History," in Bruce Kuklick and D. G. Hart, eds., *Religious Advocacy and American History* (Grand Rapids: William B. Eerdmans, 1997), 96–111, and Michael Kazin, "Howard Zinn's Disappointing History of the United States," History News Network, https://historynewsnetwork.org/article/4370. Granted, there remain a few, for instance, who insist that the Holocaust did not occur, but these remain small pockets of people with little influence. It should be added that awareness of one's operating assumptions/worldview goes a long way in protecting against sloppy work. See Eugene D. Genovese, "Marxism, Christianity, and Bias in the Study of Southern Slave Society," in *Religious*

Advocacy, ed. Kuklick and Hart, 83–95, and Wilfred M. McClay, "The Winds of History," *Touchstone: A Journal of Mere Christianity* 18 (May 2005).

[8]John Piper and Justin Taylor, eds., *A God Entranced Vision of All Things: The Legacy of Jonathan Edwards* (Wheaton, IL: Crossway Books), 2004.

[9]Piper and Taylor, *A God Entranced Vision of All Things*, 16.

[10]See the discussion in Douglas Wilson, *Five Cities that Ruled the World: How Jerusalem, Athens, Rome, London and New York Shaped Global History* (Nashville: Thomas Nelson, 2009), xvi–xx.

[11]See Nash, *Christian Faith*, 69–70.

[12]It is not uncommon to find people who believe (no pun intended) that only religious people operate in the realm of "faith." See John Warwick Montgomery, *Where Is History Going?* (Minneapolis: Bethany Fellowship, 1969), 40 and 136.

[13]See John R. W. Stott, *Your Mind Matters* (Downers Grove, IL: InterVarsity Press, 1972), 34, and Graham A. Cole, *Engaging the Holy Spirit* (Wheaton, IL: Crossway Books, 2007), 80–81.

[14]For those who hold to Protestant theology, Kant's influence in separating faith from knowledge is significant. See Nash, *Christian Faith*, 62. Also see the discussion in H. Richard Niebuhr, *Christ and Culture* (New York: Harper & Row, 1951), 110–12.

[15]Nash, *Christian Faith*, 62; emphasis in original.

[16]As quoted in Montgomery, *Where Is History Going?*, 137; emphasis in original.

[17]Esther Lightcap Meek, *Longing to Know: The Philosophy for Ordinary People* (Grand Rapids: Brazos Press, 2003), 13; also see p. 44.

[18]As quoted in Timothy Keller, *The Reason for God: Belief in an Age of Skepticism* (New York: Dutton, 2008), 120. Also see p. xvii. Keller's trenchant book is alert to the bogus nature of the sharp division between faith and reason.

[19]Ralph Waldo Emerson, *Selected Essays* (New York: Penguin Books, 1982), 123–24.

[20]Many books have been written that relate to the discussion here, but two I've read recently are highly recommended: James Davison Hunter and Paul Nedelisky, *Science and the Good: The Tragic Quest for the Foundations of Morality* (New Haven, CT: Yale University Press, 2018), and Samuel Gregg, *Reason, Faith, and the Struggle for Western Civilization* (Washington, DC: Regnery, 2019).

[21]George Ladd argued there are two valid senses of *objective*: events that are "publicly observable" and those that "actually took place in the real world outside of people's subjective consciousness." See the helpful discussion in Nash, *Christian Faith*, 114. Nash makes a persuasive case for

the "coherence view" of truth when engaging with history. See pp. 9 and 108–9.

[22]Wilfred M. McClay, *A Student's Guide to U.S. History* (Wilmington, DE: ISI Books, 2000), 9; also see pp. 4–5. Gertrude Himmelfarb offers some balanced insights in *On Looking into the Abyss* (New York: Alfred A. Knopf, 1994), 134–38.

[23]Steven B. Sample, *The Contrarian's Guide to Leadership* (San Francisco: Jossey-Bass, 2002), 64. Also see the description of the "Baconian Fallacy" in David Hackett Fischer, *Historians' Fallacies* (New York: Harper & Row, 1970), 4–8. Fischer applies the fallacy to historians, but scientists should take note as well. Make sure to check out the important work of Lesslie Newbigin, *Proper Confidence: Faith, Doubt and Certainty in Christian Discipleship* (Grand Rapids: William B. Eerdmans, 1995). At the end of the day, however, there is much we can know about historical events. See Mark Noll, "Traditional Christianity and the Possibility of Historical Knowledge," *Christian Scholar's Review* 19 (June 1990): 388–406, and John Patrick Diggins, Jackson Lears, Cushing Strout, reply by Gordon S. Wood, "Writing History: An Exchange," *New York Review of Books* 29, no. 20 (December 1982), www.nybooks.com/articles/6369. See especially the response of Gordon S. Wood.

[24]For a fine critique of Marx's faith in materialism, see Montgomery, *Where Is History Going?*, 20–21.

[25]See Allan Bloom, *The Closing of the American Mind* (New York: Simon & Schuster, 1987), 182.

[26]As quoted in Fischer, *Historians' Fallacies*, xii.

[27]See Philip Dray, *Stealing God's Thunder: Benjamin Franklin's Lightning Rod and the Invention of America* (New York: Random House, 2005), 10–11.

[28]Robert Royal, *The God That Did Not Fail* (New York: Encounter Books, 2006), 63.

[29]Scott Hahn, *A Father Who Keeps His Promises* (Ann Arbor, MI: Servant Publications, 1998), 21.

[30]As a result, some believe Christians have a decided advantage to understanding history. See Montgomery, *Where Is History Going?*, 112–13, and Kenneth O. Gangel, "Arnold Toynbee: An Evangelical Evaluation," *Bibliotheca Sacra* 134 (April–June 1977): 151.

[31]See the wise reflections of Douglas L. Wilson, "Thomas Jefferson and the Character Issue," *Atlantic Monthly*, November 1992, 1. Also see Trueman, *Histories and Fallacies*, esp. chapter 3.

[32]See Fischer, *Historians' Fallacies*, 139.

[33]Fischer, *Historians' Fallacies*,199.

[34]Joshua Wolf Shenk, *Lincoln's Melancholy: How Depression Challenged a President and Fueled His Greatness* (New York: Houghton Mifflin, 2005), 34; emphasis in original. A helpful overview of various historiographical

approaches to the study of Lincoln can be found on pp. 4–7. Also see Richard Brookhiser, "Was Lincoln Gay?," *New York Times Book Review*, January 9, 2005, 13. St. Augustine's close friendships with men is sometimes used by some to demonstrate he was gay.

[35] As quoted in Mark Dever, *Nine Marks of a Healthy Church*, new exp. ed. (Wheaton, IL: Crossway Books, 2004), 59.

[36] Himmelfarb, *On Looking into the Abyss*, 159–60; emphasis mine.

[37] See Mary Beard, *SPQR: A History of Ancient Rome* (New York: Liveright, 2015), 15–16.

CHAPTER FOUR

MOORE'S MAXIMS FOR A PRODUCTIVE LEARNING EXPERIENCE

The humble Christian is more apt to find fault with his own pride than with that of other men. He is apt to put the best construction on others' words and behavior and to think that none is as proud as he is. **—Jonathan Edwards**

By humility, he [Augustine] means not when a man, with a consciousness of some virtue, refrains from pride, but when he truly feels that he has no refuge but in humility. **—John Calvin**

This is my reply to anyone who asks: "What was God doing before he made heaven and earth?" My reply is not that which someone is said to have given as a joke to evade the force of the question. He said: "He was preparing hells for people who inquire into profundities." It is one thing to laugh, another to see the point at issue.... I would have preferred him to answer, "I am ignorant of what I do not know" rather than reply so as to ridicule someone who has asked a deep question and to win approval for an answer which is a mistake. **—Augustine**

We should have humility when discussing important issues—or any topic for that matter. Humility ought to characterize every aspect of our lives, so it certainly should inform the way we approach the study of history.

Ben Franklin had several unlikely friendships. There was the one with evangelist George Whitefield and another with well-known minister Cotton Mather. Once when Franklin was paying a visit to Mather, the famous preacher showed Franklin a shorter route out of the house. Later, Franklin reflected on the lesson he learned that day from Mather's urgent warning as they made their way out through the narrow passageway. Mather told Franklin to "Stoop! Stoop!"

Franklin was initially not clear why Mather urged him to stoop, but when Ben's head came in contact with a low beam, he gained understanding. Franklin continued with the lesson Mather gave him that day: "Let this be a caution to you not always to hold your head so high. Stoop, young man, stoop—as you go through this world—and you'll miss many hard thumps."[1]

What Is Humility?

Humility is widely misunderstood. Eighteenth-century writer William Law believed that humility is the "least understood, the least regarded, the least intended, the least desired, and the least sought after, of all virtues."[2] Some think humility is synonymous with a lack of courage or conviction. The life of Jesus demolishes such a notion. Jesus had strong convictions (it seems silly stating the obvious, but it is necessary at times) and communicated these with courage, yet he is described as "humble in heart" (Matt. 11:29 NASB). Jesus wasn't playacting at humility; humility is central to who he is. James Houston calls Jesus "the humble God."[3] There is much worth pondering in that pregnant description.

Indeed, the very idea of humility has lost its place among Christians. And many of us are unaware of the impact that Christian teachings on humility have made in our world today. John Dickson puts it well:

> But just as astonishing as the early description of Jesus as "God" is the fact that these first Christians could in the same breath say (or sing) "God" and "cross." The idea that any great individual, let alone one "in very nature God," could be associated with a shameful Roman crucifixion is just bizarre. Contemporary Christians may find the thought easy enough, but that's only because of two thousand years of reflection on this narrative. Western culture is now utterly "cruciform"—shaped by the event of Jesus's crucifixion.[4]

Another misunderstanding, and arguably the most common, is that we can never truly know when we are humble. To think you are humble, as the popular joke goes, means that you just lost any humility you may have previously possessed. Scripture alerts us to the error in this kind of thinking. First, note that there is a clear connection between humility and obedience to God (see Phil. 2:8).[5] Since humility is directly connected to obeying God, and since what obedience to God entails is clear, we can know when we are humble.[6] By submitting to God's will over our own, we manifest humility. Granted, temptations constantly lurk due to pride, but humility is hardly an elusive virtue. Furthermore, humility is commanded in Scripture (1 Pet. 5:5). If it were unclear what humility entailed, the commandment to be humble would be cruel (Mic. 6:8).

I was encouraged to discover that there are others who believe humility can be cultivated. One popular writer says that we are able to "grow in humility" and can "weaken pride and develop humility."[7] As we saw previously with William Law, *humility should be sought because it can be attained.*

Ancient Greek and Roman cultures placed no premium on humility. Personal glory, power, and aggressiveness were valued. Even in the main grouping of classical virtues (justice, courage, self-discipline, and wisdom), we find no mention of humility.

In contrast, Christians throughout the ages have trumpeted the importance of cultivating humility.[8] In Bunyan's great book *The Pilgrim's Progress*, we find a man by the name of Mr. Fearing. Mr. Fearing is not tempted by the worldliness found at Vanity Fair. Though he is uncertain about whether God has truly forgiven him (find out more by reading and rereading this brilliant and life-giving book), he greatly values humility. Mr. Fearing loves rolling around in the Valley of Humiliation. Bunyan describes the Valley of Humiliation as "the most fruitful ground." He also describes this place as "fat ground." Fruitful and fat are two *f*s worth remembering.

To cultivate any virtue, one must have a clear idea of what to do to acquire, keep, and increase it. We need not be bashful about our desire to be characterized by humility. Oswald Chambers said humility before God can be misunderstood by others. To know one's sin and to know one has been forgiven by a gracious God may seem the opposite of humility to some. Chambers instructs us not to pay any attention to such concerns. Our responsibility is to humble ourselves before God. We can entrust how people view us to God.[9]

Again, we can know when we are humble. To say otherwise is prideful, for it fails to recognize God's work of grace in our lives. Allow William Law's words to sink in deeply: "Rather, as all virtue is founded in truth, so humility is founded in a true and just sense of our weakness, misery, and sin. He who rightly feels and lives in this sense of his condition lives in humility."[10]

I vividly recall the first time I encountered the verse that describes Jesus as "humble in heart" (Matt. 11:29 NASB). It was momentous and raised all sorts of questions about how well I knew God. Since we are image bearers of this God, we ought to take seriously the call and command to be humble.

Honesty about Our Own Sin

When we are honest about our own sin, it helps us to be more long-suffering with the struggles of others. This certainly does not mean we steer clear of confronting sin in the lives of others. Among other things, Scripture says it would be unloving to fail in this regard (Prov. 27:5–6; Matt. 18:15–20). However, a deeper appreciation of our own sin must guide the way as we consider confronting the sins of others (Matt. 7:1–5; Gal. 6:1).[11] This is helpful to remember in reading history, especially when we are reading about someone whose behavior is easy to judge in some ways. This does not mean we should move in the opposite direction and never render any kind of assessment about the actions of others. It does mean that we remember our own flaws as we read about the flaws of others.

Henri Nouwen taught at Notre Dame, Yale, and Harvard. He left Harvard for L'Arche, a community ministering to "mentally handicapped" men and women. Nouwen moved, in his words, "from the best and the brightest, wanting to rule the world, to men and women who had few or no words and were considered, at best, marginal to the needs of our society."[12] How was Nouwen able to make such a radical transition? Nouwen understood better than most that he himself was weak and broken.

There are many benefits that come from living humbly before God and others. Thomas à Kempis underscored such things as wisdom, peace, and what I like to call "stability of spirit."[13] He understood that deep change can seem elusive and warned against the compulsion many had to make pilgrimages. He said these hardly ever change someone for the better—another reminder that there is nothing new under the sun. Think here of the drive many Christians have to hurry up and attend the latest conference. Kempis sought to get at the roots of our problem, which lie in the disordered passions of the human heart. He offered a searching meditation on pride. It is uncomfortable to hear what Kempis said, but it clarifies a lot about the human predicament.

Remember, Only God Is Omniscient!

I have many good memories of my times at Dallas Theological Seminary and Trinity Evangelical Divinity School. At each school, there were teachers who humbly acknowledged what they did not know. Two examples stand out—both were willing to learn from their students.[14] I vividly recall both professors pausing at times during lectures to register thanks for things they themselves were learning from their pupils.

In contrast, a cynic thinks he knows it all. Cynics can't be humble because they have determined there is nothing left to learn which could change their bleak assessment of things. Their minds are made up. They see no need to learn anything. The folly of coming to such a conclusion is poignantly addressed in the classic movie *It's a Wonderful Life*. The lead character, George Bailey (played by Jimmy Stewart), believes his life is of no value and so decides to commit suicide. Just in the nick of time, a guardian angel reveals the myriad of ways George's life has positively impacted others. George Bailey really did have a "wonderful life." The pessimism of the deeply depressed Bailey was misplaced.

There is one thing I have noticed in every healthy person I've known, and I'm not talking here about those who have physical well-being but instead what some like to call "whole persons." People who are healthy have a bias that there is much they do not know and/or have not experienced. This gives them an attractive strength of character, makes them insatiably curious, and gives them a keen awareness that there is much left to learn. These kinds of people rarely, if ever, complain of boredom.

Listening . . . A Lost Art

Some people seem to find it rather challenging to listen well. John Adams noted this particular trait about New Yorkers: "They talk very loud, very fast, and altogether. If they ask you a question, before you can utter three words of your answer, they will break out upon you again—and talk away."[15] My wife, who was raised in northern New Jersey, a mere stone's throw away from Manhattan, warned me about this phenomenon during my first trek for family gatherings at her parents' place. There were extended family members from New York, and the rest hailed from New Jersey. I assure you there is no demonstrable difference between the two states when it comes to listening. I remember walking into a room and hearing almost everyone talking *at the same time.* My wife, who seeks to be a good listener, graciously coached me in some coping strategies.

In college, I recall a study that demonstrated how poorly most of us listen. The plant in the experiment would casually make contact with someone in the fruit section of a grocery store. After a few pleasantries were exchanged, the plant would say the following with great joy: "My mother died." Nine out of ten people responded, "That's great." Most people obviously did not hear the words but simply took their cues from the exuberance of the plant.

Listening well is a characteristic of humble people. Listening well is also crucial to investigating the past. Sifting through a time period to determine with some accuracy what occurred is not easy. It requires the willingness to persevere and not inflict one's biases on the record of the past. Truly listening to let others tell their stories is a necessary discipline when learning history well.

Moore's Maxims

There are several things to keep in mind when we discuss important and, many times, controversial matters. This certainly entails the study of history. Things can get heated when people interact regarding what happened in the past. Just try broaching the issue of whether the United States was founded as a Christian nation or whether American exceptionalism is a good idea with no real drawbacks.

Over my many years of teaching, and hopefully being more honest with my own sin, there are four principles I have developed that undergird my own approach.

Principle 1

First, in times of conflict, it is possible that we did not properly understand the other person's position. We may be jumping the proverbial gun and thus setting up a straw man argument. A great antidote, and one we have just noted that is characteristic of humble people, is listening well. We should make certain we are properly tracking what is communicated. We are told in

Scripture to be "quick to hear, slow to speak, and slow to anger" (James 1:19 NASB).

The Christian teaching on hell has occupied most of my adult life. My thesis and then first book was on hell.[16] I have spent much time thinking on the subject, working through Scripture, and struggling with the nature of God's judgment.

Some of you may be familiar with the folks from Westboro Baptist Church. They are the ones who like to show up with signs announcing that some person or group is "going to hell." The people of Westboro Baptist think they are being brave by proclaiming the scandalous message that people who do not trust Christ are going to hell. When I consider their actions, the following illustration comes to mind. I think it illumines the folly of the approach of those who align with Westboro Baptist; it also highlights their inability to listen well.

Most people have not been to either Yuma, Arizona, or Dubrovnik, Croatia. I have been to both locations. Yuma is a fine place. There are some quaint things to see there, but Dubrovnik is absolutely stunning in its beauty. Now let's say I offer someone an all-expenses-paid trip to either Yuma or Dubrovnik. Most would have to guess which one is better because they don't know anything about these places, beyond perhaps hearing their names. I have heard the television show *Game of Thrones* was filmed in Dubrovnik, but if you are like me and don't watch the show, you would remain uncertain about where to go. There is simply no context for determining whether the offer of Dubrovnik or Yuma is preferable.

The folks at Westboro jump right to the topic of hell, but there are so many important biblical truths to know before one can even begin to appreciate hell. I have found many church-going folks need more background on the character of God, the nature of sin, and so forth, to better understand Scripture's teaching on hell. If that is true of regular church attenders, it is certainly more so with those who know little of the Christian faith. Listening well and making sure others understand what is being said is not a strength of the folks at Westboro Baptist Church.

Principle 2

The second principle relates to how well we understand our own position. The most secure in any debate are those who have taken time for adequate preparation. Our need here is to dig deeper and see if, in fact, our position holds up. Christian growth, as we talked about earlier in this book, is tied directly to our growth in knowledge. And this comes from recognizing when we really don't know what we are talking about. We can learn something especially important here from the ancient philosopher Socrates. The Oracle of Delphi said he was the wisest man in all of Athens. Socrates thought the pronouncement was over the top and so sought to demonstrate that it was untrue. He assumed, rightly he thought, that there were others wiser than he. Like a good investigative reporter, he sought out several people. It turned out that everyone acted wise but were, in fact, rather foolish. Socrates ended up accepting that the "oracle's declaration was actually correct, for at least he recognized his own ignorance."[17]

It is also interesting to note Augustine's admiration for a non-Christian teacher by the name of Faustus:

> I wanted Faustus to tell me, after comparing the mathematical calculations which I had read in other books,

> whether the story contained in the Manichee books was correct, or at least whether it had an equal chance of being so. I now did not think him clever enough to explain the matter. Nevertheless I put forward my problems for consideration and discussion. He modestly did not even venture to take up the burden. *He knew himself to be uninformed on these matters and was not ashamed to confess it. He was not one of the many loquacious people, whom I have had to endure, who attempted to instruct me and had nothing to say.*[18]

Principle 3

Third, we may properly understand the other person's position as well as our own but give them more importance than they deserve. We typically do this in one of two ways: by making a secondary (or even tertiary) issue into a primary one, or by failing to remember that there are gray issues that sincere Christians disagree over (see 1 Cor. 8; Rom. 14). I am not on Twitter or Facebook but have observed in both places that this principle is violated on a regular basis. In fact, all four of my principles are constantly violated on social media.

Principle 4

Finally, we may properly understand the other position and our own, it may be an important issue, but we still need to communicate with grace and truth. Again, having a gracious spirit does not mean there must be a toning down of one's convictions. It does mean we proceed cautiously, ever aware of our own fallen and finite state.[19] We must be vigilant to guard against a nasty or demeaning posture toward those who disagree with us.

Benefits to You and Your Ministry

I recently discovered a fascinating lecture series sponsored by the Aspen Institute. It featured two MDs, Jerome Groopman and Pamela Hartzband. Both teach at Harvard Medical School. It is important to note that Groopman and Hartzband are married to one another.

I knew about Dr. Groopman because of his blockbuster book *How Doctors Think*. Among other things, the discussion at the Aspen Institute revolved around some of the themes in that book.

Groopman described what it was like to come from an Eastern European Jewish background that revered scientists and doctors. People like Jonas Salk were held in high regard. Groopman's community during his formative years would defer to people from the scientific and technological sectors of society. Other areas of study were not given nearly as much respect. Groopman said his community gave unflattering labels to those in villages who believed things outside the narrow domains of science and technology. As a result, Groopman labels himself a "maximalist believer" when it comes to opting for medical intervention.

Groopman's wife grew up in a very different type of home. She labels herself a "minimalist doubter" when it comes to medical intervention. Hartzband's mother had the correct instinct to buck her own doctor's recommendation of a rigid breastfeeding regimen. Her mom was not a doctor or scientist but simply followed her own inclinations. She believed (and her experience seemed to back it up) that breastfeeding her child more frequently was better than adhering to set feeding times. Both of Hartzband's parents exercised on a regular basis and ate well. Because of these experiences, Hartzband grew up in a family where other disciplines were valued, beyond just medical intervention.

Both Groopman and Hartzband have top-flight training. (They obviously could not be teaching at Harvard without it.) Both are keenly aware that they can diagnose the same patient and come up with different plans of how to proceed. When colleagues ask Hartzband how quickly surgery ought to be scheduled for a patient, she has a "wait and see" approach. Groopman has a different approach. He is much quicker to put the patient "under the knife."

What's fascinating is that both of these doctors agree that the new metrics-driven decision-making in medicine is disastrous. Both emphasize that many things are not reducible to numbers. They also underscore that some doctors are better at diagnosis while others are better at doing the actual procedure. A bad situation would see those two doctors inverted.

What does this have to do with the study of history? Quite a bit, actually. The study of history reminds us that there are many dynamics at work. History teaches us to appreciate these many factors and not privilege one area over another. Yes, there are important people, but there are also ideas that bubble up from lesser lights. Yes, environment can affect history. Just think of how changes in environment have impacted innumerable wars, both in terms of when they were fought and how. And yet history is not reducible to a changing climate. History teaches us to be patient, listen better, and embrace that our world is far more complex than many of us typically think. In other words, history is a great boon to humility.

History helps us to be "self-consciously thinking about *how* we are thinking *as* we are thinking."[20] All of us can stand to benefit from being more attentive to why we think in the ways we think. Granted, this is unsettling—that's why it is so rare. Putting ourselves in a vulnerable place where our thinking is open to evaluation is scary. Those who want to mature in their thinking know the risks are worth it. We should also have wise friends who are willing to probe our beliefs. And they should allow us to return the favor.

There are various ways people try to make sense of the world. Some think a number-crunching approach is the most useful. We can certainly grant that statistics do offer some illumination, but being without a story to tell, there are limits to the usefulness of a purely quantitative approach.

W. E. B. DuBois was the first Black man to earn a doctorate from Harvard. He "pioneered a new method of social science research that had become a hallmark of the Progressive Era reform: the social survey."[21] But even though it was cutting edge at the time, it did not tell a story. When DuBois saw the body parts of a lynched man for sale in a store window, he realized that social surveys could not describe such outrage. He knew from that point on that "one could not be a calm, cool and detached scientist while Negroes were lynched, murdered, and starved."[22]

In his inimitable way, William F. Buckley liked to say, "Quantitative analysis, you beautiful doll!"[23] We must be careful, lest we get overly snookered by the appeal of numbers. In a wonderful essay titled "The Maniac," G. K. Chesterton said mathematicians, in an effort to make sense of a complex world, tend to go mad when they realize this is an impossibility. Chesterton said that chess players and cashiers have the same problem. Then there are poets. Poets are quite comfortable with a world they can't fully comprehend. Chesterton went on to say this is why many mathematicians and their related ilk are found among the insane, whereas the population of poets in what Chesterton called "lunatic asylums" was low. Chesterton was no advocate for irrationality. He makes that clear in the essay. He exaggerated to make his point but articulated an important truth.

Though Chesterton was comparing the differences between how poets and mathematicians try to make sense of the world, the broad point also applies to those who value history and those who don't. Good history reminds us that there are, in fact, real things that took place in time and space. These events, as I have already said, are things we can know with a great deal of confidence. This confidence, however, is not at odds with being surprised, corrected, and humbled by what we may discover. History does get revised to various degrees, but most of what we know about the past does not get radically retold. For example, there are fringe groups who try and deny the Holocaust, but these views never gather much of an audience.

Holy, Humble, *and* Humorous People

My good friend Roger asked me to give him two character qualities that quickly come to mind when I think of a godly person. Without much thought, I blurted out the words *holy* and *humble*. An additional *h* word, a sense of *humor*, is not the kind of thing we tend to think of when it comes to holy and humble people, but it really should be added.

Terry Lindvall is the author of a terrific book on the "comic world" of C. S. Lewis. Lindvall has some wise words to offer about the place of humor and its relationship to humility:

> A proud man cannot laugh because he must watch his dignity; he cannot give himself over to the rocking and rolling of his belly. But a poor and happy man laughs heartily because he gives no serious attention to his ego. The proud person may at best smile like Buddha, with the controlled half-smile of moral or psychological superiority. Yet it is one of the vices of our culture that we honor and commend the smile in sophisticated or polite company and save the laughter for more common arenas. Even Confucius warned, "Beware the man whose belly does not move when he laughs."[24]

Lindvall says that "humor and humility should keep good company. Self-deprecating humor can be a healthy reminder that we are not the center of the universe, that humility is our proper posture before our fellow humans as well as before almighty God."[25] In my interview with Lindvall, he insightfully unpacked how the opposite of humor is not seriousness but tragedy, thus indicating a way to discuss serious matters with (appropriate) humor.[26]

Christian philosopher Søren Kierkegaard also had something to say about the connection between humor and Christian piety:

> His [Kierkegaard's] point is that since humorists spend much time pointing out absurdities in life, they are well prepared to embrace the absurd aspects of (in Kierkegaard's judgment) the Christian life. Such aspects of doctrine might be better described as paradoxical or ironic, but Kierkegaard's point still stands . . . *it suggests that an important aspect of wit—humility—is also crucial for faith. Which by itself might be sufficient reason to take humor seriously.*[27]

This is a wonderful reminder as we close. My desire is that your study of history (whether it is newfound or ongoing) will be marked by a holy and humble confidence in the truth, and that you will not lose sight of the ironic or humorous, because history is, as David McCullough likes to remind us, loaded with human beings.

Discussion Questions

1. How should an appreciation of our own sin influence our posture when we have a disagreement with someone over an important topic? For example, even Christians hold different views on whether Lincoln was a great president. What do Christ-like convictions look like during such times?

2. Should a disagreement with a Christian over a secondary doctrine (e.g., predestination versus the "free will" of man) be handled any differently than a disagreement with a skeptic over a primary doctrine (e.g., the deity of Christ)?

3. When Jesus called the Pharisees a "brood of vipers" (Matt. 23:33 NASB), he was still full of "grace and truth" (John 1:17 NASB). What would this look like in our own lives?

4. How has your perspective on humility been changed as a result of reading this chapter? How might it affect your study of history?

Notes

[1] As quoted in Walter Isaacson, *Benjamin Franklin: An American Life* (New York: Simon & Schuster, 2003), 41.

[2] William Law, *A Serious Call to a Devout and Holy Life* (Philadelphia: Westminster Press, n.d.), 104.

[3] James M. Houston, *The Mentored Life* (Colorado Springs: NavPress, 2002), 50.

[4] John Dickson, "How Christian Humility Upended the World," Australian Broadcasting Company (ABC), October 27, 2011.

[5] I am grateful to my good friend Judge Thomas Wright, who (forty years ago!) first got me thinking about this connection.

[6] We see humility displayed by Jesus in submitting fully to the Father's will (see John 5:19–20). Of course, Jesus's submission to the Father is epitomized in the Garden of Gethsemane.

[7] C. J. Mahaney, *Humility: True Greatness* (Sisters, OR: Multnomah, 2005), 22 and 65. Also see p. 169.

[8] See the insightful observations of J. Oswald Sanders, *Spiritual Leadership*, rev. ed. (Chicago: Moody Press, 1980), 23.

[9] Oswald Chambers, *My Utmost for His Highest* (New York: Dodd, Mead, 1963), 335.

[10] Law, *A Serious Call to a Devout and Holy Life*, 105.

[11] If we are in touch with our own sin, we will not be harsh with others. See Thomas à Kempis, *The Imitation of Christ*, trans. William C. Creasy (Notre Dame: Ave Maria Press, 1989), 1:2 and 2:5. Also see Chambers, *My Utmost for His Highest*, 174.

[12] Henri J. M. Nouwen, *In the Name of Jesus* (New York: Crossroads, 1994), 11. This short book is chock full of wise and candid insights about the struggle to humble oneself before others.

[13] See Kempis, *Imitation of Christ*, 1:4, 1:7, 2:2, and 3:7.

[14] Here I am thinking of Dr. Fred Howe, professor of theology at Dallas Theological Seminary, and Dr. Wayne Grudem, who now teaches at Phoenix Seminary.

[15] As quoted in McCullough, *John Adams*, 25.

[16] David George Moore, *The Battle for Hell: A Survey and Evaluation of Evangelicals' Growing Attraction to the Doctrine of Annihilationism* (Lanham, MD: University Press of America, 1995).

[17] James S. Spiegel, *How to Be Good in a World Gone Bad* (Grand Rapids: Kregel, 2004), 176.

[18] Augustine, *Confessions*, trans. Henry Chadwick (New York: Oxford University Press, 1991), 5.7; emphasis mine.

[19] For a terrific reflection on George Eliot's *Middlemarch*, especially with respect to our limited perspectives, see David F. Ford, *The Drama of Living: Becoming Wise in the Spirit* (Grand Rapids: Brazos Press, 2014), 56.

[20] Robert Tracy McKenzie, *A Little Book for New Historians* (Downers Grove, IL: InterVarsity Press, 2019), 58.

[21] Jill Lepore, *These Truths: A History of the United States* (New York: W. W. Norton, 2018), 370.

[22] Lepore, *These Truths*, 370.

[23] William F. Buckley Jr., *Let Us Talk of Many Things: The Collected Speeches* (Roseville, CA: Forum, 2000), 17.

[24] Terry Lindvall, *Surprised by Laughter: The Comic World of C. S. Lewis* (Nashville: Thomas Nelson, 1996), 131.

[25] Lindvall, *Surprised by Laughter*, 133.

[26] David George Moore, "Moore about Faith," on KIXL radio, May 16, 1998.

[27] Spiegel, *How to Be Good*, 133; emphasis mine. For two terrific introductions to Kierkegaard, see Mark Tietjen, *Kierkegaard: A Christian Missionary to Christians* (Downers Grove, IL: InterVarsity Press, 2016), and Stephen Backhouse, *Kierkegaard: A Single Life* (Grand Rapids: Zondervan, 2016).

APPENDICES

Appendix A includes three interviews I have done for *Patheos/Jesus Creed*. They cover controversial and important historical events. They also showcase how careful historical thinking should be done.

Appendix B contains a short journal article I wrote about twenty years ago. It seeks to demonstrate why historical literacy is critical for reading the Bible responsibly. My gratitude to the *Patheos/Jesus Creed* blog and the *Reformation & Revival* journal for granting me the rights to include these in this book.

APPENDIX A

INTERVIEWS

Robert Tracy McKenzie

The First Thanksgiving
What the Real Story Tells Us about Loving God and Learning from History

The following interview demonstrates how history can be used irresponsibly, especially when it covers a subject we thought we "knew so well."

Robert Tracy McKenzie is a professor and chair of history at Wheaton College. He taught for many years at the University of Washington, where he was the holder of the Donald W. Logan Endowed Chair in American History. He is the author of *One South or Many? Plantation Belt and Upcountry in Civil War-Era Tennessee* (Cambridge University Press) and *Lincolnites and Rebels: A Divided Town in the American Civil War* (Oxford University Press). He blogs at http://faithandamericanhistory.wordpress.com.

The following interview with Professor McKenzie centers around his book *The First Thanksgiving: What the Real*

Story Tells Us about Loving God and Learning from History (InterVarsity Press, 2013).

Moore: What was the spark that motivated you to write this book?

McKenzie: There were two, really. At the most foundational level was a new sense of vocation. After two decades of writing primarily for other specialists in my field (which is what scholars in the academy are trained to do and rewarded for doing), I began to sense a call to write more directly for the church, to enter into conversation with believers on the question of what it means to love God with our minds. More directly, the inspiration for this book was an invitation from my church several years ago to give a talk on the first Thanksgiving. In preparing for it, it dawned on me that the topic was a wonderful way to engage Christians interested in history and broach crucial questions in the process. I don't think I've ever met someone interested in history who was first drawn to the past by a piece of dry academic scholarship. What initially captivates us are the stories. I came to realize that the story of the first Thanksgiving, retold faithfully, raises all kinds of important questions about what it means to think "Christianly" about the past.

Moore: Mark Noll points to the incarnation of Jesus as a key reason why Christians ought to seek to understand the past. Would you elaborate a bit on Noll's observation?

McKenzie: In *Jesus Christ and the Life of the Mind,* Noll writes, "If it is true that the Word became flesh, it must be true that the realm that bore the Word, the realm of flesh, is worthy of the most serious consideration." In other words, the incarnation of

Jesus gives great dignity to the material world and to the human story that Jesus became a part of and identified with. Elsewhere, Noll has observed that, if we take seriously the Christian teaching that God is sovereign over history, then there is a sense in which the unfolding of human history is a part of his revelation to mankind. This strikes me as another powerful reason for giving careful attention to history.

Moore: True education, as the ancient Greeks understood it, is painful. It is painful because true education causes us to confront truths that necessarily force us to reevaluate our cherished beliefs. So, I wonder, since you are writing about the cherished beliefs of Christians, how many have gotten angry at you for what you wrote?

McKenzie: No one has attacked me yet, but that may be because the folks most likely to be offended haven't read it yet. By and large, Christian historians stopped writing for Christians outside the academy long ago, so if Christians in the pews are a bit suspicious of us, we have given them reason to be so. This is why one of the things I tried to do in the book was to identify myself openly and immediately as an evangelical Christian. This will not spare me from criticism from Christian readers, but I did want readers to think of me as coming alongside them rather than confronting or admonishing them. Beyond this, I did my best to explain that my motive in writing the book was not primarily to "debunk," to underscore all the ways that our popular memory of the first Thanksgiving is wrong. Rather, I am convinced that the mythical past we have created obscures aspects of the Pilgrim story that would bless us greatly. The truth is richer, more challenging, more potentially life changing than the stereotypes we learned in grade school.

Moore: What are a few of the biggest misconceptions about the "first Thanksgiving"?

McKenzie: The ones that we tend to get hung up on are not very important. For example, most of how we envision the event in our mind's eye would never hold up in court. There is no conclusive evidence that the Pilgrims ate turkey and pumpkin pie, that they celebrated in November, or that they invited the local Native Americans to join in their feast. (It's at least as likely that the Wampanoag showed up uninvited.) At the same time, I don't think much is lost by our remembering the event in that way.

Far more serious, I think, is how we have totally lost sight of the mindset that the Pilgrims brought to the table. Indeed, I would say that the two most important things we have forgotten about the Pilgrims are also the two most elementary: how they understood Thanksgiving, and what they meant when they called themselves "pilgrims." I note in response to another of your questions that the Pilgrims feared that a regularly scheduled Thanksgiving could easily become an empty ritual. And indeed, several generations would pass before their descendants would begin to observe an annual autumn Thanksgiving.

With regard to pilgrimage, we have lost the original meaning of that concept. When William Bradford wrote that "they knew they were pilgrims," he meant that they were acutely conscious of the fact that this world was not their home. Bradford was quoting from the eleventh chapter of the book of Hebrews, where the writer tells us that the great heroes of the faith had this in common, that they knew that they were strangers and pilgrims in this world, and sought as their ultimate home a heavenly country. We tend to remember the Pilgrim story today as if their promised land was the future United States.

Moore: Your respect for the Pilgrims is clear. What are a few things you appreciate most about them?

McKenzie: The Pilgrims had their blind spots—as do we—but there is much in their example we can learn from. They were men and women of deep conviction, uneasily daunted, willing to suffer for principle's sake. They loved their children, they loved the body of Christ, and they abandoned everything that was familiar to them in order to serve both. They exhibited enormous *courage*: can you imagine cramming 102 passengers into a ship's hold the size of a school bus and making a sixty-five-day voyage to a strange world? Having taken that initial step of faith, they then *persevered* in the face of unspeakable hardship and loss, with half of the colony dying from exposure that first winter. Because the *Mayflower* stayed at Plymouth until the spring of 1621, the survivors could have returned to England, but none did. Finally, they exhibited a *faith* in God's sovereignty that humbles me. What we remember as the "first Thanksgiving" was a celebration primarily of widowers and orphans. (Fourteen of the eighteen wives who made the voyage had died by spring.) That the Pilgrims could celebrate at all in this setting was a testimony both to human *resilience* and to heavenly *hope*.

Moore: Unpack what you meant when you wrote, "At its best, the study of history always involves a simultaneous encounter with both the familiar and the strange."

McKenzie: Basically, this is the idea that the people whom we encounter in the past will be like us in some ways and different from us in others. We may see the differences as quaint or mildly amusing, but rarely will we see them as relevant to our lives. One of the things that I argue in the book is that we need to pay much more attention to the ways in which historical figures were different from us. It is in wrestling with those differences that we have an opportunity to be challenged by the past, maybe even to learn from the past something we desperately need. One of the reasons we so seldom take the strangeness of the past seriously is that we all too often go to the past already knowing what we want to find. This is the pitfall that I label the "history-as-ammunition" approach—where we approach the past looking for supporting evidence for a position we already hold. Sadly, we can never learn anything at all from the past when that is our motivation.

Moore: It will undoubtedly surprise many to find out that the Pilgrims were suspicious of almost all regular holidays. Would you describe that a bit for us?

McKenzie: Sure. We can begin to understand by taking the term "holiday" seriously—the word is an elision of the two words "holy day." A holiday was a day set apart for sacred religious observances. Second, we need to understand that the Pilgrims believed that the Catholic Church had wrongly invented countless rites and rituals not explicitly prescribed in Scripture, and they were determined not to duplicate this perceived error. As a result, they resolved not to recognize any holiday not authorized scripturally. As they read the Bible, they believed that only three such holidays were clearly authorized.

The first was the Sabbath, which of course was to be observed regularly, fifty-two times a year. The other two holidays were to be observed only irregularly in response to extraordinary judgments or blessings of God. The first was a Day of Fasting and Humiliation. The second was a Day of Thanksgiving. (In seventeenth-century Massachusetts, holy days of Fasting and Humiliation were called about twice as frequently as days of Thanksgiving.) Finally, the Pilgrims believed that, like most human inventions, a regularly scheduled holiday could easily become a meaningless ritual.

Moore: What can American Christians learn from the importance the Pilgrims placed on group identity?

McKenzie: This would be an example of taking the strangeness of the past seriously. The Pilgrims did not think of society as made up of a conglomeration of autonomous individuals. Rather, they thought in terms of groups: family, community, church. (The first laws of Plymouth did not even allow single men to live by themselves; they were assigned to live in households.) We often remember the Pilgrims as coming to America "in search of religious freedom." As I point out in the book, the Pilgrim writers make clear that they experienced extensive religious toleration in Leiden, Holland, where they had settled after leaving England. What they stressed instead was "the hardness of the place," in William Bradford's words, by which he meant the great economic hardships that were their lot there. But even though they desired a home with greater economic opportunity, it would be misleading to think that they were primarily looking for a home where each individual could maximize his or her welfare. Indeed, Bradford is clear that many members of the Leiden congregation had been considering leaving Leiden because they were suffering so, and the search for a home in the Americas was primarily driven by the hope of keeping their congregation together. When we take this aspect of the Pilgrims' worldview seriously, it helps us to see as with new eyes the rampant individualism of contemporary American culture that we take for granted.

Moore: One question I have asked many writers is how they capture their research. Would you give us an overview of your own approach?

McKenzie: Aarrgh! I don't think I would be a model for anyone, as I am both slow and inefficient. If I own a book or document, I mark it up extensively while I am reading it. When I have finished reading it, I take out my laptop and, without looking at the document, I type out a very quick overview, summarizing the nature of the document; its author, context, and reliability; and its main points. (I do this as an exercise to improve recall, but I can't swear that it works in my case.) Finally, I refer to the document and flesh out the main points with fuller notes. For a book like this one, in the end I will have several hundred pages of typed notes and comments.

Moore: Speculate a bit about how you think David Barton would review your book.

McKenzie: That's a tough one. He and I have never met, although I have read several of his books. I want to be careful in responding. I admire David Barton's zeal and his courage, and given that I have spent a great deal of my professional life focused solely on the Academy, I respect his determination to reach out to a broad audience of Christian readers. And I would hope that, if Barton should read my book, he would at least recognize in me a Christian brother who sincerely wants to serve the body of Christ. At the same time, if he were to read the book perceptively, he would have to find much that is troubling (and I would hope, convicting). To be candid, I think that Mr. Barton violates most of the principles that I advocate for thinking Christianly about the past. He ignores the strangeness of the past, he goes to the past for ammunition rather than enlightenment, and he teaches about the past in a way that promotes arrogance more than humility.

Moore: Thanks for taking the time to write such a terrific book! What are some of your future book projects?

McKenzie: I am considering a variety of possibilities. What I know for sure is that I want to continue to try to be in conversation with Christians outside the walls of the Academy. One possibility is a book of meditations on the American Civil War, a cataclysm that was saturated with eternal questions. I've also long wanted to write a book on the rise of American democracy in the form of a series of vignettes. Finally, although it is not a book, I would absolutely love to create a video course on American history for Christian schools and home schools.

Jemar Tisby

The Color of Compromise
The Truth about the American Church's Complicity in Racism

Jemar Tisby is the author of the much-talked-about book *The Color of Compromise* (Zondervan). Tisby serves as president of The Witness: A Black Christian Collective, cohosts the *Pass the Mic* podcast, and is a doctoral candidate in history at the University of Mississippi.

Moore: I've been thinking much of late how C. S. Lewis and George Orwell both believed that words are powerful. You write that "complicity" is not an adequate word to depict the lack of involvement among Whites when it comes to race. Would you unpack that some for us? I'm also curious why you still chose to use "complicity" in the title of your book and even regularly throughout the book.

Tisby: Further down in that same paragraph I explain, "Even if only a small portion of Christians committed the most notorious acts of racism, many more White Christians can be described as complicit in creating and sustaining a racist society." So, complicity is a weak word when describing the most extreme and violent manifestations of anti-Black racism. I needed to express the idea that "complicity" would not be adequate to describe *all* White Christian responses in the face of racism. There were plenty of people who claimed to love God but hated their neighbors of color and maliciously acted on that animosity. But the vast majority of Christians, especially laypeople, simply exhibited willful ignorance, apathy, or silence in face of racial atrocities. In this sense, then, complicity is an accurate word to describe the great mass of "moderate" Christians whose inaction permitted a society based on racial stratification to form.

Moore: Your book is clear and convicting. Among White audiences, what are some of the most encouraging things you've heard about the book?

Tisby: After a talk I gave about the book, a person who described himself as a "sixty-year-old White man from the South" came up to me with tears in his eyes and said the book was helping him overcome the truncated and distorted view of race and history that he had learned. On countless other occasions, White Christians have sent me messages telling me how they've used the book as conversation starters with relatives and friends. Older Black Christians who lived through much of the hard history I tell in the book hug me in appreciation for helping to communicate their story. I love hearing stories about groups gathering to discuss the book in community. Most encouraging, my niece who is in third grade did a book report about *The Color of Compromise*. I had to learn much of this history as an adult, so I'm glad that younger generations can access this information long before I did.

Moore: You've spent a lot of time thinking about this issue, not only because of the research for this book but also because you are in the midst of a PhD program in history. Can you highlight a few things that surprised you in your research, or possibly altered your thinking in some way?

Tisby: The ubiquity of racism has given me pause. I've read hundreds of academic books on history and in every single field—labor, gender, politics, military, etc.—race always figures prominently. It disappointed me to observe that almost every time historians highlighted Christianity and race, followers of Christ, at least those with the most social and ecclesiastical power, were almost always on the wrong side of justice.

Not just the breadth but also the depth of racism in the church took me aback. From the moment Christopher Columbus contacted Native Americans, paternalistic ideas of race were at the forefront. He evaluated indigenous people only based on how well they could assimilate to European culture (including their version of Christianity) and what kind of servants they might make. In 1667, the Virginia Assembly made a law reassuring slaveholders that baptism would not emancipate an enslaved person. That's more than a century before the political entity known as the United States of America came into being. So, there was never a "great" period of American history when race was not a problem. It is the depth and breadth of racism in the nation and the church that filled me with godly anger and a desire to broadcast these truths to a wider audience in hopes of change.

Moore: How does the separation of the church from so-called political matters affect the issues revolving around race in America?

Tisby: Separating racial issues from the gospel makes it easy for churches and individual Christians to sidestep this pernicious problem. If racism is mainly a civil or political issue, then Christians have no obligation to intervene. Historically, Christians have used doctrines such as the "spirituality of the church" to play the role of Pontius Pilate and wash their hands of racism. But Christians in this nation cannot downplay their complicity in racism. History is rife with the receipts. In addition to the perpetuation of a racist status quo, the effect of such conflict avoidance is that Black Christians have chosen to separate themselves from their spiritual brothers and sisters who seem unconcerned about the injustices racism has heaped upon Black communities both past and present. A refusal to embrace a holistic gospel that includes social justice has kept the body of Christ divided along racial and theological lines.

Moore: As you well know, there has been a statement decrying "social justice" that was signed by many evangelical leaders. What, if anything, did they get wrong?

Tisby: The so-called statement on social justice and the gospel got too many things wrong to name them all. Stepping back from the actual document, the intention itself is open to critique. In my estimation, the writers and signatories have responded to an imagined enemy. They have taken the most extreme forms of ideology and transposed them onto brothers and sisters in Christ. They have accused me and others of replacing the gospel with Communist, Marxist ideas of collectivism. I am simply a student of history. When you see how Christians acted in racist ways in spite of, and sometimes because of, their religious beliefs, it leads to certain conclusions about racial struggles and what to do about them. Studying history compels you to focus not just on isolated acts of racial animus but to pay attention to the ways our entire society has been built upon notions of racism and White supremacy.

In general, White Christians think very individualistically overall and especially when it comes to race. Race relations in the church would improve exponentially if more people understood the systemic and institutional manifestations of racism and then acted to counteract those forces.

Moore: It seems that the hyper-individualized understanding of faith among conservative Christians can blind us to the reality of "structures of evil." What have you found to be most helpful in persuading Christians to consider the reality of structures of evil?

Tisby: I actually think we need to spend a bit less time persuading recalcitrant Christians about the reality of systemic and institutional racism. There is a small but vocal and increasingly aggressive contingent of Christians on the blogosphere and social media who not only resist the idea of structural racism, they attack those who see the issue differently. These people leech away time and energy from more profitable pursuits. I recommend Christians spend more time advocating for the marginalized than attempting to persuade those who merely want to argue. These are spiritual issues, and one must exhibit a level of humility to learn about the ways racism continues to affect the church and the nation, especially if it is a reality that goes against a long-held narrative about how race functions.

That said, there are those who may not agree that structural racism is an issue, but they are open to learning more. In those cases, I start with sources they already trust. So, of course, the Bible is at the top of the list. I point to passages such as Leviticus 19:15, Deuteronomy 16:19, Ezekiel 22:29, and many other verses that speak of injustice occurring on a system-wide level. I also point to other sources such as denominational resolutions about race and confessions of faith that explain the practical implications of biblical commands. From there I move on to other sources such as books on history and sociology.

A last word on persuading Christians about systemic and institutional injustice. . . . White Christians have a great responsibility to help educate other White people in their networks about this issue. Many Black Christians will never have the same level of access or trust with White people that other White people have. We will not be able to talk to your uncle or grandmother, your roommate, or coworker, but you can. In those moments, when only White people are around but another White person chooses to interrupt racism, those are the times when some of the most important antiracist work happens.

Moore: What are two or three things you hope your readers will take from this book?

Tisby: I hope people understand at least these two themes: First, racism never goes away; it just adapts. Second, it didn't have to be this way. If racism is sin, which it is, then we should expect that it will never completely disappear until Jesus returns. But if one's concept of racism is limited to people donning white robes and hoods and burning crosses on lawns, then you will be tempted to think that racism is largely a problem of the past and relatively rare in the present. Racism has not gone away. It has just gone underground. We must have our ears attuned to the dog whistles, and sometimes bullhorns, politicians use in their rhetoric. We need to peel back the layers of inequality and ask how racism has excluded scores of people from opportunities. It's there if we have eyes to see.

It didn't have to be this way. Historians often talk about the concept of "contingency." It's the idea that historical circumstances are full of dependent variables. Small changes here or there could have resulted in different outcomes. When it comes to race, this means that a racist society was not inevitable. Although racism is entrenched now, there have always been alternatives when individuals could have made different decisions, more just and equitable ones, that would have led to less racist conditions. This points to the last idea I hope people take away from *The Color of Compromise.* If it didn't have to be this way in the past, then it doesn't have to be this way in the future. We have the opportunity right now to make different and better decisions when it comes to race in the church. We can commit to forging a more racially just future for our children and the household of God. We can refuse to practice a complicit Christianity and instead choose to practice a courageous Christianity.

James McPherson

The War That Forged a Nation
Learning about the Catastrophic Civil War

The following interview with Pulitzer Prize winner James McPherson addresses a time period everyone has something to say about. It is also an area of study in which McPherson is considered one of the leading experts.

McPherson is widely viewed as one of the foremost living scholars of the Civil War era. His book *Battle Cry of Freedom* (Oxford University Press) won the Pulitzer Prize and has sold more than 700,000 copies. Many other books have come from McPherson's gifted pen (and then followed by his trusty Olympia typewriter).

McPherson has won many awards for his work. Along with the Pulitzer Prize, he has received the Lincoln Prize and the Pritzker Literature Award for Lifetime Achievement in Military Writing.

McPherson is the George Henry Davis 1886 Professor of American History, Emeritus, at Princeton University.

The following interview revolves around McPherson's latest book, *The War That Forged a Nation* (Oxford University Press).

Moore: At the beginning of your book, you mention the spectacular success of the PBS documentary on the Civil War by Ken Burns. Recently, I heard Civil War historian Gary Gallagher level some criticism about that documentary. As you well know, other historians have also weighed in with their own concerns. What are your thoughts about the portrayal of the Civil War found in that documentary?

McPherson: I also have a couple of criticisms of the Ken Burns documentary, but they are not necessarily the same as those by some of my colleagues. The narrative script had a substantial number of minor factual errors—no single one of them would have merited criticism, but the cumulative effect marred the presentation. Ken should have submitted the script to a careful reading by a couple of Civil War scholars. Secondly, some of the photographs did not illustrate the particular events being described by the narrative—they were of another event or scene entirely. Only those who were familiar with the photographs would have picked up on this, but these (relatively few) cases also were jarring.

At the same time, however, I think some of the criticisms canceled each other out: some southerners found it too "pro-Northern"; others found it "too Southern." Some found that it emphasized slavery too strongly; others that it paid too little attention to slavery as an issue that caused the war and that the war had to address. Another criticism is that it largely ignored Reconstruction, and focused instead in the final episode on postwar reconciliation between veterans of the blue and gray. I don't agree with these criticisms—the purpose of the series was to present to a large television audience, only a fraction of which was greatly knowledgeable about the Civil War, the story of that titanic and momentous conflict. The series succeeded spectacularly in achieving that purpose. It aroused the interest of millions of viewers, many of whom went on to learn more about the war by reading books and articles, visiting battlefields, and the like. This in itself was a great boon to Civil War studies.

Moore: What is the significance of the "United States" going from a plural noun to a singular one?

McPherson: Before the war, the words "United States" were usually construed as a plural noun. Local and state governments touched the lives of the average person much more closely than the national government; the identity and allegiance of most people was to their state or region more than to the nation. The United States was a rather loose federation of states; the Bill of Rights was a restraint on the powers of the national government in favor of state and individual rights. Nationalism existed, as was proved in the crisis of 1861, but the experience of war greatly strengthened it. The North went to war in 1861 to preserve the *Union,* but came out of the war as a unified *nation* in which the national government was far more powerful in 1865 than it had been four years earlier. In the generation after the war the United States *was* (not *were*) on *its* (not *their*) way to becoming a world power.

Moore: Did both the North and South believe themselves to be following the direction of the Founding Fathers of our country?

McPherson: Both the Union and Confederacy wrapped themselves in the mantle of 1776 and 1787, and professed to be fighting for the ideals and institutions established by the founding fathers. Just as the revolutionaries of 1776 claimed to be seceding from the tyranny of the British crown and Parliament, the Southern disunionists of 1860–1861 claimed to be seceding from the potential tyranny of a federal government under Abraham Lincoln and his party. But Lincoln and the Northern people fought to preserve the creation of the American republic from dismemberment and ruin, and therefore to preserve the legacy of 1776. Confederates claimed to fight for the Constitution of 1787 with its protection of slavery and state rights; Northerners professed to fight to defend that Constitution from the destruction that would be the result of the breaking up of the Union that the Constitution had created.

Moore: Andrew Delbanco of Columbia has famously said that Americans believed in the providence of God before the Civil War and then in luck as they surveyed the war's aftermath. Seeing the scale of carnage rattled many people. How much does the Civil War still shape the American consciousness about God and country?

McPherson: During the war, most people on each side believed that *God was on their side*. Confederate defeat shook this faith in the South, to be sure, but the emergence of a "Lost Cause" mentality in the decades after the war, which championed the idea that the Confederacy had fought nobly, even though they were overpowered by the godless North, helped reconcile them to defeat. In the North, victory reinforced their faith in the righteousness of their cause; the continuing popularity of Julia Ward Howe's "Battle Hymn of the Republic" has sustained that conviction right on down to the present. Lincoln famously argued that God had his own purposes in the war, of which the most important was to punish *all* White Americans, Northern as well as Southern, for the sin of slavery. As Lincoln himself acknowledged, that was not a popular idea then, and perhaps is not popular today, but the recognition that the war purged the nation of the guilt of slavery that had made a mockery of its claim to be "the land of the free" has helped to inspire American nationalism ever since the war.

Moore: My own marginalia by your discussion of McClellan's leadership is "presumption, paranoia, and pride." If my three *p*s are somewhat accurate, could we say that Grant is somewhat of the antithesis to McClellan?

McPherson: The notion that Grant's personality and leadership were the opposite of McClellan's "presumption, paranoia, and pride" is an excellent one. In all of these respects, Grant indeed was the opposite of McClellan. He worked his way up from colonel of an Illinois regiment to general-in-chief of the United States armies step by step, earning these promotions by achievement rather than favor. He never expressed jealousy of fellow officers or criticism of his superiors in the paranoiac manner that McClellan did, and he was modest about his success in contrast to McClellan's exaggerations of his limited successes and boasting (in letters to his wife) about them. McClellan blamed others for his failures while Grant took responsibility for decisions (as at Cold Harbor) that resulted in failures.

Moore: Lincoln evokes strong emotions among Americans. Opinions about him range from our greatest president to characterizations bordering on the demonic. How high do you rank Lincoln's presidency and why?

McPherson: I would rank Lincoln's presidency as the most important in American history, or at the least, equally important as George Washington's. Washington's leadership launched the nation; Lincoln's saved it from dissolution and purged it of the curse of slavery that Washington and the other founders had been unable to eliminate from their new nation. Much of the criticism of Lincoln has focused on his alleged violations of civil liberties during the war, but in fact these violations were considerably less than those of the Woodrow Wilson administration during World War I and the Franklin D. Roosevelt administration during World War II, even though the dangers from internal dissension in a civil war were greater than those during foreign wars. Lincoln managed to lead the nation through a crisis that preserved its national integrity and ended slavery, and he did so in a manner that also preserved democratic institutions.

Moore: Much has been written about the Civil War. What are a few areas (people, ideas, or events) that have not been well covered?

McPherson: So much has been written about the Civil War that it is hard to identify areas or individuals that have not been well covered. Two areas that have received some treatment but would profit from more are the environmental impact of the war and the story of refugees in the South. How serious was deforestation of large parts of Virginia, for example, or the marching, camping, fighting, and marauding of armies over thousands of square miles of farmland and woodlands? How long did it take the environment to recover? With respect to refugees, how many people were uprooted by the war? How many families left home to escape the ravages of war? How many of them died? What about slaves fleeing their homes in search of freedom? Is it possible to estimate the numbers of refugees, Black as well as White, during the war? What about mortality among them? We know something about the mortality of Blacks in contraband camps, but what about Southern Whites who took to the roads? The current focus on refugees fleeing the Middle East and Africa suggests that a more intensive study of refugees during the chaos of war in 1861 to 1865 might add an important dimension to our understanding of the war.

APPENDIX B

RAISING SOME CONCERNS OVER THE "INDUCTIVE METHOD" OF BIBLE STUDY

A Brief Sketch of Its History[*]

In college, I learned a method of studying the Bible that was immensely helpful. A few years later while attending Dallas Theological Seminary, I honed my understanding of an approach to Bible study popularly called the "inductive method." The threefold process of observation, interpretation, and application/correlation was extremely valuable to learn. I continue to believe that it is a good approach to Bible study *as long as certain considerations are kept in mind.* My concern over the teaching and learning of the inductive method, however, is that important cautions and clarifications are not typically given. The result of learning this particular method of Bible study without the proper perspective can give a misplaced confidence in how clearly God's Word speaks on some doctrinal themes/

---

[*]This article first appeared in the pages of the *Revival & Reformation* journal, Fall 2000. Kind permission to include it here was granted by Dr. John Armstrong, editor. It seeks to demonstrate why reading only your Bible can be a dangerous thing.

issues.[1] A brief look at church history will hopefully illustrate these concerns.[2]

During the medieval period, Peter Lombard (ca. AD 1100–1160) wrote his famous theological work *Book of Sentences* (AD 1158). Lombard's work was the first major attempt to use "the logical method to arrive at a definition of orthodoxy." He sought to give a "coherent, objective statement of Christian belief."[3] *Book of Sentences* was the major theological text used by candidates in theology at European universities until Aquinas's *Summa Theologica* replaced it during the seventeenth century. It is noteworthy to observe that from Lombard and Aquinas "modern theology derives its systematic urge."[4]

The study of theology in the Western church also moved from the monasteries to the universities during the medieval period. Theology increasingly became a *separate* discipline that one studied in the university classroom.

In the Eastern tradition, theology has never left the monasteries and churches. Theology is learned in a worshiping environment, not as a separate field of inquiry. In the Orthodox tradition, there is a popular saying that "[t]he rule of prayer is the rule of belief and action."[5] In other words, there is no dichotomy between what one "knows" and what one does with that knowledge.[6] In the Western tradition of the church, we find a spate of *systematic* theologies. In the East, there is clearly a reticence about organizing the Scriptures in this sort of logical fashion.[7]

During the Renaissance, Francis Bacon developed what became known as "the inductive method." The age of modern science had arrived. Proving something to be true involved tests that utilized skills such as carefully observing data, interpreting one's findings, and applying the conclusion to the world at large. Conclusions were understood to be tentative at times. Many times they were working assumptions that others challenged and eventually refuted. One thinks here of the discoveries of Galileo and Copernicus in upending long-held "conclusions" about the physical universe.

Later, the Enlightenment presented a new challenge to the Christian faith. We think of the assaults of thinkers like Voltaire and others. These skeptics believed that the Christian tradition was antiquated, even dangerous. They could point to wars that were spawned by religious passions. The Thirty Years' War (1618–48), which some highlight as a series of wars, was one very recent example that they could readily point out. Millions died. Instead of the destructive power of superstitious religious tradition, *autonomous*[8] human *reason* was understood to bring the "good life." People didn't need to submit to any authority, especially religious ones. Even where the concept of a deity was still invoked, it turned out that he was made in the image of the philosophers.

> Human reason, operating by means of careful observation and checking its conclusions by further observation or experiment, could for the first time in the history of man reveal the mechanism of the natural world in which he had lived for so long like a fearful and wondering child. Nature, instead of being a mere collection of phenomena, a hotchpotch [alternative spelling of hodgepodge] of occult influences or the canvas on which an inscrutable Providence painted its mysterious symbols, was a system of

> intelligible forces. *God was a mathematician whose calculations, although infinite in their subtle complexity, were accessible to man's intelligence.*[9]

In the middle of the nineteenth century, there were other events that put the church on the defensive. The challenges of Darwinian evolution and German higher criticism resulted in varied responses from the church. Some Christians decided to remove themselves from the scholarly debates. Forsaking the fray, these Christians built their own protective environments in which to shield themselves. Evangelical subcultures kept the heretics from encroaching and thereby polluting sacred territory.

Other Christians chose to challenge the hegemony of scientific rationalism to any authority, especially attacks on religious ones. Many of these believers were heroic in their efforts. The value they placed on the scientific method, however, was sometimes misguided. For instance, the same year that Darwin's *Origin of Species* came out, a book titled *Organon of Scripture* or *The Inductive Method of Biblical Interpretation* was published. The author, James S. Lamar, confidently proclaimed, "The Scriptures admit of being studied and expounded upon the principles of the inductive method, and . . . *when thus interpreted they speak to us in a voice as certain and unmistakable as the language of nature heard in the experiments and observations of science.*"[10] Many well-intentioned Christians wanted to show that the Christian faith was just as rational as, or even more rational than, any other philosophy or religious viewpoint.[11] As these debates wore on into the twentieth century, it was not uncommon to see Christian theologians say,

"Systematic Theology is the collecting, scientifically arranging, comparing, exhibiting, and defending of *all* facts from any and every source concerning God and his works."[12]

The philosophy of "Common Sense Realism" also had an impact on the Christian understanding of Scripture. Simply stated, this is the view that sought to answer the skepticism of David Hume by saying that human beings have the innate ability to perceive reality accurately without any significant distortion. Though some have argued that "Common Sense Realism" was the main reason for the modern church holding to the doctrine of inerrancy, others have shown that inerrancy has always been the historic position of the church.[13] Notwithstanding this possible error of chalking up inerrancy solely to the influence of "Common Sense Realism," we do see how the strong confidence placed in reason affected the study of theology. Conservative scholars at Princeton Seminary provide one example:

> The apparent contradiction between Princeton's trust in Common Sense [Realism] and its adherence to the doctrine of universal human sinfulness had little effect on these professors' assertions about the scientific character of theology. In his introduction to *Systematic Theology* (1872), Charles Hodge had argued that the theologian should strive to be just as scientific as the chemist or astronomer. "The Bible is to the theologian what nature is to the man of science," he wrote. "It is his storehouse of facts." In similar terms, Warfield, who like Hodge before him was the chief name at Princeton, claimed that the theologian needed to think through and organize Christian

> teaching not merely in order to defend it but to attack opposing views. Christianity, he argued, "had been placed in the world to reason its way to the dominion of the world."[14]

These historical events are briefly described to show why we Western Christians would have a natural penchant to latch onto the inductive method of Bible study as the method of choice. Our fondness for systematization, reason, and 100 percent certitude causes us to be more interested in methods that promise clarity and confidence.

Let me tease out some implications:

1. It is historical naivete and intellectual pride to think that the inductive Bible study method is the best or only way to familiarize oneself with God's Word. The Eastern Orthodox tradition employs other methods. Even the Western Christian tradition has utilized other approaches like *lectio divina*[15] that self-consciously rely more on meditation, thoughtful reading,[16] and prayer. James Houston has wisely said, "Over some sixteen centuries *lectio divina* has proved itself capable of transforming the reader in a remarkably long-lasting and institutionalized tradition."[17]

2. It is impossible to be totally detached and completely objective[18] in studying anything—science or theology.[19] We all have assumptions about life and God that color our view of Scripture.[20] This is clearly a strong warrant for a growing and mature understanding of church history. We must acquaint ourselves with what other Christians have believed throughout the sweep of church history. The profound arrogance and destructiveness of believing that "all that I need is the Bible" has

shown itself on many sad occasions.[21] In fact, Professor Howard Hendricks, from whom I learned the inductive method of Bible study, would say while holding his own Bible in the air, "If this is the only book you ever know, you will never know this book."

3. Realizing that theological systems are human constructions should lead neither to skepticism on one hand nor to pride on the other. Mark Noll states the proper balance:

> It must be remembered that truth about God is absolute in the sense of being true without exception. It does not change. Thus, when the Bible speaks of God and this is the source of doctrines, these doctrinal truths can be stated in a final form. However, caution must be exercised, since doctrinal statements are the interpretive constructions of man and so capable of including error, of being inadequately conceived or stated. They are also capable of growth as the church's knowledge of the Scripture grows. So while truth is certain and absolute, men's knowledge of truth is not in every case equally absolute or final.[22]

4. *Sola Scriptura* does not mean that we discount the role of tradition. It simply means that the Bible is the ultimate and final authority. For example, Wesleyans have a very helpful way to remember this in their quadrilateral. Scripture is the ultimate and final authority, but reason, church history (tradition), and even experience can provide checks on how well we may have understood God's Word.[23]

5. It is fine to use color-coded pencils and make charts of the Bible. They clearly have their place as aids to bolster memory, but we need to keep in mind how seriously they can be abused.

If one gets the idea after charting a certain book of the Bible that he now *completely* understands it, his confidence in what the inductive method has accomplished is misplaced. For example, when people study 1 Thessalonians with the inductive method and conclude that dispensational premillennialism is "the only reasonable position because it is so clear and compelling," it is time to remind them that many godly and scholarly Christians beg to differ. Proponents of other eschatological positions make the same error as well.

6. We must be careful what our expectations are with respect to the Bible. If the Bible is believed to be merely a "how to" book, we will grow impatient with sections that don't easily lend themselves to simple application points on how to have a terrific marriage or how to raise great children. The Scriptures, of course, have much practical advice on these and other topics, yet the Bible is much more than a "how to" manual.

Since all of Scripture is inspired by God (2 Timothy 3:16), it is incumbent that we familiarize ourselves with *all* of it. This keeps us balanced in the best sense of that word (Acts 20:26–27).

Because the inductive method puts application in such a prominent position (rightly, I believe), it is important to state explicitly that all the Bible is important, even if certain parts do not lend themselves to easy applications. It is this latter point that could be spelled out more clearly when the inductive method is taught.

It is my experience from hearing the inductive method taught that the teachers will voice a desire that others discover for themselves what the Scriptures say. This is all well and good. Unfortunately, there are too many times when this encouragement to be a "Berean" (ironically a commonly misinterpreted verse) is contradicted by the teacher's impassioned plea that a particular theological system or position is *clearly* the correct one.

I continue to teach the inductive method of Bible study and find it to be quite helpful. It needs, however, to always be accompanied by a clear *caveat lector*.[24]

Notes

[1] The clarity of Scripture refers to cardinal doctrines like the deity of Christ, not to secondary, and certainly not to tertiary, doctrines.

[2] This article certainly does not purport to be the final word on this important topic. There are many more avenues for further study and reflection. This is simply an attempt to highlight *some* of the significant issues.

[3] Walter A. Elwell, ed., *Evangelical Dictionary of Theology* (Grand Rapids: Baker, 1984), s.v. "Peter Lombard," by R. G. Clouse.

[4] Ellen T. Charry, *By the Renewing of Your Minds: The Pastoral Function of Christian Doctrine* (New York: Oxford University Press, 1997), 230. A similar observation can be found in Leon J. Podles, *The Church Impotent: The Feminization of Christianity* (Dallas: Spence, 1999), 110–11.

[5] As quoted in Daniel B. Clendenin, ed., *Eastern Orthodox Theology: A Contemporary Reader* (Grand Rapids: Baker, 1995), 7.

[6] There is no dichotomy in the Western tradition at its best either.

[7] Daniel B. Clendenin, *Eastern Orthodox Christianity: A Western Perspective* (Grand Rapids: Baker, 1994), 53. This does not mean to diminish the reality of substantial biblical scholarship taking place in the Orthodox tradition. Anyone who is familiar with this tradition knows that this is patently not the case.

[8] Literally, this means "self-law." My adaptation of this word, which is tragically apropos for our modern age, is "self as law. "

[9] Norman Hampson, *The Enlightenment* (New York: Penguin Books, 1968), 37–38; emphasis mine.

[10] As quoted in Christopher A. Hall, *Reading the Scripture with the Church Fathers* (Downers Grove, IL: InterVarsity Press, 1998), 25–26; emphasis mine.

[11] I have heard this said by many ministers and confess that I am guilty of saying it myself.

[12]Lewis Sperry Chafer, *Systematic Theology*, vol. 1 (Dallas: Dallas Seminary Press, 1947), x. I am grateful for Christopher A. Hall's fine book *Reading the Scripture with the Church Fathers*, which jogged my memory of this quote.

[13]The best treatment is John D. Woodbridge, *Biblical Authority: A Critique of the Rogers/McKim Proposal* (Grand Rapids: Zondervan, 1982).

[14]As quoted in D. G. Hart, *Defending the Faith: J. Gresham Machen and the Crisis of Conservative Protestantism in Modem America* (Grand Rapids: Baker, 1995), 25. The original sources are Charles Hodge, *Systematic Theology*, vol. 1 (Grand Rapids: Baker, 1975), 10, and Benjamin Breckinridge Warfield, "Introduction to Beattie's Apologetics," reprinted in *Selected Shorter Writings of Benjamin B. Warfield*, vol. 2, John E. Meeter, ed. (Phillipsburg, NJ: Presbyterian & Reformed, 1973), 99.

[15]For a helpful introduction to this approach, see Diogenes Allen, *Spiritual Theology* (Boston: Cowley, 1997).

[16]One friend sheepishly asked me if it was "okay" to just slowly read and meditate on Scripture. Guilt nagged her because she did not naturally gravitate toward the inductive method. I allayed these fears by informing her that I rarely use the inductive method, even for sermon preparation.

[17]James M. Houston, "Toward a Biblical Spirituality," in *The Act of Bible Reading*, ed. Elmer Dyck (Downers Grove, IL: InterVarsity Press, 1996), 161.

[18]Lest the reader think that I am fascinated by the irrationality of various "postmodern" methodologies, I am not. I simply want to underscore that the Christian faith is neither modern nor postmodern. It is premodern.

[19]Michael Polanyi has done some groundbreaking work in this regard. I am indebted to Lesslie Newbigin, *Proper Confidence: Faith, Doubt & Certainty in Christian Discipleship* (Grand Rapids: William B. Eerdmans, 1995), 39–44, for introducing me to Polanyi.

[20]Though deconstructionism is wrongheaded, it does remind us that we study texts as subjects/persons. The subjective element in Bible study cannot be totally eliminated. In other words, robotic detachment and complete objectivity are an impossibility.

[21]One thinks of examples like Victor Paul Wierwille, founder of The Way International. Fed up with intramural theological debates, Wierwille took his theological library of more than three thousand volumes to the city dump. Shortly thereafter, he denied the cardinal doctrines of the Christian faith.

[22]Mark A. Noll, "Who Sets the Stage for Understanding Scripture?," *Christianity Today* (May 23, 1980): 16. I am grateful to the following book, which gave me the quote by Noll: Elliot E. Johnson, *Expository Hermeneutics: An Introduction* (Grand Rapids: Zondervan, 1990), 288.

[23]See Allen Coppedge, "How Wesleyans Do Theology," in *Doing Theology in Today's World*, ed. John. D. Woodbridge and Thomas Edmund McComiskey (Grand Rapids: Zondervan, 1991), 267–89.

[24] I am grateful to Warren Culwell, Mike Field, Colby Kinser, Dr. Robert Pyne, Barbara Miaso, and my wife, Doreen, for various input and assistance on earlier drafts of this article. They certainly bear no responsibility for the finished product. I sent copies of this article to Professor Howard Hendricks of Dallas Theological Seminary and Kay Arthur of Precept Ministries. Both of their busy schedules prohibited any feedback.

SUGGESTED READING

Bendroth, Margaret. *The Spiritual Practice of Remembering.* Grand Rapids: William B. Eerdmans, 2013.

Fea, John. *Why Study History? Reflecting on the Importance of the Past.* Grand Rapids: Baker Academic, 2013.

Fischer, David Hackett. *Historians' Fallacies: Toward a Logic of Historical Thought.* New York: Harper & Row, 1970.

Himmelfarb, Gertrude. *On Looking into the Abyss: Untimely Thoughts on Culture and Society.* New York: Alfred A. Knopf, 1994.

McClay, Wilfred M. *A Student's Guide to American History.* Wilmington, DE: ISI Books, 2000.

McKenzie, Robert Tracy. *The First Thanksgiving: What the Real Story Tells Us about Loving God and Learning from History.* Downers Grove, IL: InterVarsity Press, 2013.

———. *A Little Book for New Historians: Why and How to Study History.* Downers Grove, IL: InterVarsity Press, 2019.

Montgomery, John Warwick. *Where Is History Going?: A Christian Response to Secular Philosophies of History.* Minneapolis: Bethany Fellowship, 1969.

Nash, Ronald H. *Christian Faith and Historical Understanding*. Grand Rapids: Zondervan, 1984.

Niebuhr, Reinhold. *The Irony of American History*. Chicago: University of Chicago Press, 2008.

Trueman, Carl R. *Histories and Fallacies: Problems Faced in the Writing of History*. Wheaton, IL: Crossway Books, 2010.

ABOUT THE AUTHOR

Dave is the founder and president of Two Cities Ministries in Austin, Texas. He's had many jobs from arresting shoplifters to pastoral ministry. The latter was the most dangerous.

He is the author of four books. Dave's commentary on Ecclesiastes was picked by *Preaching Magazine* as "one of the year's best books for preachers." His articles have appeared in the Austin *American-Statesman, Bibliotheca Sacra, Current Thoughts & Trends, Front Porch Republic, The Gospel Coalition, Huffington Post, Knowing & Doing* (C. S. Lewis Institute publication), *Mere Orthodoxy, Patheos, Reformation & Revival Journal, Stulos Theological, TomPaine.com,* and *Touchstone*. He is a regular contributor to *Christianity Today/Jesus Creed,* and the C. S. Lewis Institute.

Dave's eBook *Pooping Elephants, Mowing Weeds: What Business Gurus Failed to Tell You* was published in 2018. His book *Stuck in the Present* reflects thirty years of thinking on the formative nature of lifelong learning, with a keen eye to knowing history. He is coauthoring (with Michael Haykin) a forthcoming book on Jonathan Edwards and Ralph Waldo Emerson.

He has spoken in France, Poland, Canada, Croatia, and Mexico. In the United States, he has been a plenary speaker for the Veritas Forum and Campus Crusade for Christ. Along with many retreats and conferences, Dave has given several chapel messages for NFL football teams, major league baseball groups, and the LPGA.

Media work includes interviews on TV and radio, a three-year stint as the host of a radio show, and interviewing William F. Buckley for a one-hour special, which aired nationally on PBS. He is currently writing and hosting a documentary on those who are disillusioned with organized Christianity in America.

Dave has interviewed over two hundred writers, leaders, and scholars. Among others, these include three Pulitzer prize winners.

Dave received an MA (with honors) in biblical studies from Dallas Theological Seminary and an MA in Christian Thought (*magna cum laude*) from Trinity Evangelical Divinity School. At Trinity, he was the recipient of various honors, including the Professor C. B. Bjuge Award given by the faculty for the best thesis in theology, along with being the corecipient with his wife of the Kitty DeBaets Memorial Award for commitment to "scholarship and family." During the summer of 2016, he was appointed a Visiting Scholar at Princeton Theological Seminary.

He is married to Doreen, a *summa cum laude* graduate of Trinity Evangelical Divinity School, whose book *Good Christians, Good Husbands?* is used as a regular resource at Dallas Theological Seminary. Doreen has been a Visiting Scholar at Princeton Theological Seminary.

ROOTS

Unconvering Why We Do What We Do In Church

DYRON DAUGHRITY

ISBN: 9780891123972 · $ 15.99

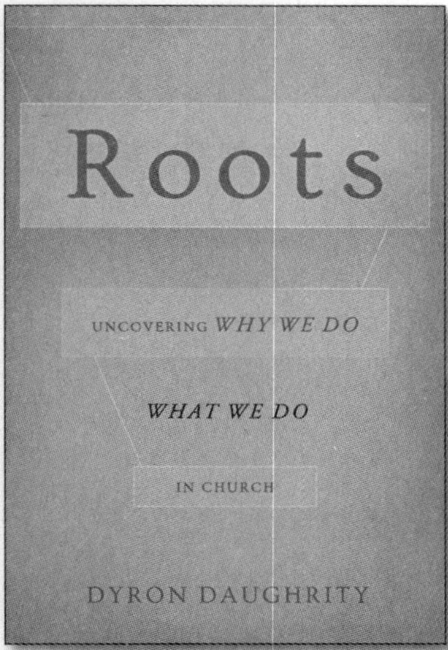

Why do we do what we do in church? Roots *answers that question. You will discover for yourself the history of seven important topics that are at the very heart of what it means to be a Christian.*

Every Christian needs to know these things and decide what they believe. By uncovering "why we do what we do in church," Christians can make more informed decisions about where they should take their churches in the future.

"When you first open Roots*, you might initially think you are getting a simple primer to Christian life and practice. Only when you delve a little further do you realize just how smartly the author identifies and confronts the key questions facing all denominations, and how deep and wide-ranging are the scholarly resources with which he tackles them. This is a truly deceptive book, and admirably so. And an enjoyable read throughout."*

—**Philip Jenkins,** Distinguished Professor of History, Institute for Studies of Religion, Baylor University

DYRON DAUGHRITY (PhD University of Calgary) has authored ten books and numerous articles on the study of religion. He is an academic editor for three international presses and is a professor of religious studies at Pepperdine University in Malibu, California.

LEAFWOOD
PUBLISHERS
an imprint of Abilene Christian University Press